THE 10 BEST

KNIFE FIGHTING
TECHNIQUES

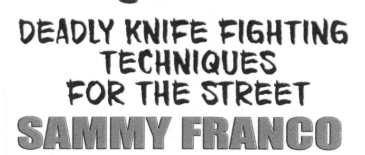

DEADLY KNIFE FIGHTING
TECHNIQUES
FOR THE STREET

SAMMY FRANCO

Also by Sammy Franco

Cane Fighting
Double End Bag Training
The Heavy Bag Bible
The Widow Maker Compendium
Invincible: Mental Toughness Techniques for Peak Performance
Unleash Hell: A Step-by-Step Guide to Devastating Widow Maker Combinations
Feral Fighting: Advanced Widow Maker Fighting Techniques
The Widow Maker Program: Extreme Self-Defense for Deadly Force Situations
Savage Street Fighting: Tactical Savagery as a Last Resort
Heavy Bag Workout
Heavy Bag Combinations
Heavy Bag Training
The Complete Body Opponent Bag Book
Stand and Deliver: A Street Warrior's Guide to Tactical Combat Stances
Maximum Damage: Hidden Secrets Behind Brutal Fighting Combinations
First Strike: End a Fight in Ten Seconds or Less!
The Bigger They Are, The Harder They Fall
Self-Defense Tips and Tricks
Kubotan Power: Quick & Simple Steps to Mastering the Kubotan Keychain
Gun Safety: For Home Defense and Concealed Carry
Out of the Cage: A Guide to Beating a Mixed Martial Artist on the Street
Warrior Wisdom: Inspiring Ideas from the World's Greatest Warriors
War Machine: How to Transform Yourself Into a Vicious and Deadly Street Fighter
1001 Street Fighting Secrets
When Seconds Count: Self-Defense for the Real World
Killer Instinct: Unarmed Combat for Street Survival
Street Lethal: Unarmed Urban Combat

The 10 Best Knife Fighting Techniques (10 Best Series #11)
Copyright © 2017 by Sammy Franco
ISBN: 978-1-941845-52-3
Printed in the United States of America

Published by Contemporary Fighting Arts, LLC.
Visit us Online at: **SammyFranco.com**

For author interviews or publicity information, please send inquiries in care of the publisher.

II

Contents

"He will win who knows when to fight and when not to fight."

– Sun Tzu, The Art of War

Warning!

The intent of this book is to provide general information about knife fighting techniques for personal self-defense and to help define areas of knife training that the reader may choose to further investigate. This program is for academic study only.

Moreover, the author, publisher and distributor do not intend for any of the information contained in this book to be used for criminal purposes. This book is about an art form and should be viewed as such.

The techniques, tactics, methods, and information described and depicted in this book can be dangerous and could result in serious injury and or death and should not be used or practiced in any way without the guidance of a qualified self-defense instructor.

The following is meant to supplement a safe edged weapon-training program. Never practice knife training without the supervision of a qualified knife-fighting instructor. Never, ever practice with sharpened or live blades. This book is for information purposes only. Please consult with local laws in your area concerning the practice of martial arts, knife sparring, and ownership or carrying of simulated weapons.

Knife fighting training is dangerous. The author, publisher, and distributors of this manual will accept no responsibility, nor are they liable to any person or entity whatsoever for any injury, damage, or loss of any sort that may arise out of practicing, teaching, or disseminating of any techniques or ideas contained herein. You assume full responsibility for the use of the information in this program and agree that the author, distributor and contributors hold no liability to you for claims, damages, costs and expenses, legal fees, or any other costs incurred due to or in any way related to your reliance on anything derived from this program or its contents.

Additionally, it is the reader's responsibility to research and comply with all local, state, and federal laws and regulations pertaining to the possession, carry, and use of edged weapons. This program is for educational reference information only!

The use of a knife or edged weapons denotes the use of deadly force and is subject to the laws of each state or local jurisdiction. Readers must assume all liability for their subsequent actions and edged weapon practices. The author, publisher, distributor and all product providers assume no liability for any actions made by readers of this program.

Before you begin any exercise program, including those suggested in this manual, it is important to check with your physician to see if you have any condition that might be aggravated by strenuous exercise.

About this Book

The 10 Best Knife Fighting Techniques: Deadly Knife Fighting Techniques for the Street is a concise guide designed to teach some of the most practical and effective knife fighting techniques for self-defense.

All of the skills featured in this book are simple and can be readily used by young and old, regardless of size or strength and level of experience. Most importantly, you don't need martial arts training to master many of these devastating knife fighting techniques.

Unlike other knife fighting books, The 10 Best Knife Fighting Techniques is devoid of impractical and gimmicky techniques that can get you injured or possibly killed when faced with a real-world self-defense crisis. Instead, this book arms you with the most efficient, effective, and practical knife fighting skills that work in the chaos of a real-world survival situation. In fact, the self-defense skills and techniques found within these pages are straightforward and easy to apply.

Practitioners who regularly practice the knife skills and techniques featured in this book will establish a rock solid foundation for using a knife for self-defense. Moreover, the techniques featured in this book will significantly improve your overall personal protection skills, enhance your conditioning, and introduce you to a new and exciting method of self-defense.

The 10 Best Knife Fighting Techniques is based on my 30+ years of research, training and teaching reality-based self-defense and combat sciences. In fact, I've taught these unique knife fighting skills to thousands of my students, and I'm confident they can help protect you and your loved ones during an emergency self-defense situation.

I also encourage you to read this book from beginning to end, chapter by chapter. Only after you have read the entire book should you treat it as a reference and skip around, reading those chapters that directly apply to you

Finally, the information, techniques, and suggestions contained herein are dangerous and should only be used to protect yourself or a loved one from the immediate risk of unlawful injury. Remember, the decision to use a knife for self-defense must always be a last resort, after all other means of avoiding violence have been exhausted.

Be safe!

Sammy Franco
SammyFranco.com

Introduction
Contemporary Fighting Arts

Exploring Contemporary Fighting Arts

Before diving head first into this book, I'd like to first introduce you to my unique system of fighting, Contemporary Fighting Arts (CFA). I hope it will give you a greater understanding and appreciation of the material covered in this book. And for those of you who are already familiar with CFA, you can skip to the next chapter.

Contemporary Fighting Arts® (CFA), is a state-of-the-art combat system that was introduced to the world in 1983. This sophisticated and practical system of self-defense is designed specifically to provide efficient and effective methods to avoid, defuse, confront, and neutralize both armed and unarmed assailants in a variety of deadly situations and circumstances.

Unlike karate, kung-fu, mixed martial arts and the like, CFA is the first offensive-based American martial art that is specifically designed for the violence that plagues our cruel city streets. CFA dispenses with the extraneous and the impractical and focuses on real-life street fighting.

Every tool, technique and tactic found within the CFA system must meet three essential criteria for fighting: efficiency, effectiveness, and safety. Efficiency means that the techniques permit you to reach your combative objective quickly and economically. Effectiveness means that the elements of the system will produce the desired effect. Finally, Safety means that the combative elements provide the least amount of danger and risk for you - the fighter.

CFA is not about mind-numbing tournaments or senseless competition. It does not require you to waste time and energy practicing forms (katas) or other impractical rituals. There are no

3

theatrical kicks or exotic techniques. Finally, CFA does not adhere blindly to tradition for tradition's sake. Simply put, it is a scientific yet pragmatic approach to staying alive on the streets.

CFA has been taught to people of all walks of life. Some include the U.S. Border Patrol, police officers, deputy sheriffs, security guards, military personnel, private investigators, surgeons, lawyers, college professors, airline pilots, as well as black belts, boxers, and kick boxers. CFA's broad appeal results from its ability to teach people how to really fight.

It's All In The Name!

Before discussing the three components that make up Contemporary Fighting Arts, it is important to understand how CFA acquired its unique name. To begin, the first word, "Contemporary," was selected because it refers to the system's modern, up-to-date orientation. Unlike traditional martial arts, CFA is specifically designed to meet the challenges of our modern world.

The second term, "Fighting," was chosen because it accurately describes the system's combat orientation. After all, why not just call it Contemporary Martial Arts? There are two reasons for this. First, the word "martial" conjures up images of traditional and impractical martial art forms that are antithetical to the system. Second, why dilute a perfectly functional name when the word "fighting" defines the system so succinctly? Contemporary Fighting Arts is about teaching people how to really fight.

Let's look at the last word, "Arts." In the subjective sense, "art" refers to the combat skills that are acquired through arduous study, practice, and observation. The bottom line is that effective street fighting skills will require consistent practice and attention. Take, for example, something as seemingly basic as an elbow strike, which will actually require hundreds of hours of practice to perfect.

The pluralization of the word "Art" reflects CFA's protean instruction. The various components of CFA's training (i.e., firearms training, stick fighting, ground fighting, natural body weapon mastery, and so on) have all truly earned their status as individual art forms and, as such, require years of consistent study and practice to perfect. To acquire a greater understanding of CFA, here is an overview of the system's three vital components: the physical, the mental, and the spiritual.

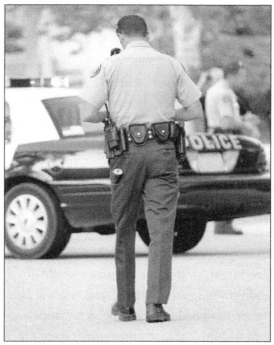

Police officers need practical and effective defensive tactics for dealing with violent street criminals. This is why many law enforcement officers seek out Contemporary Fighting Arts training.

The Physical Component

The physical component of CFA focuses on the physical development of a fighter, including physical fitness, weapon and technique mastery, and self-defense attributes.

Physical Fitness

If you are going to prevail in a street fight, you must be physically fit. It's that simple. In fact, you will never master the tools and skills of combat unless you're in excellent physical shape. On the average, you will have to spend more than an hour a day to achieve maximum fitness.

In CFA physical fitness comprises the following three broad components: cardiorespiratory conditioning, muscular/skeletal conditioning, and proper body composition.

The cardiorespiratory system includes the heart, lungs, and circulatory system, which undergo tremendous stress during the course of a street fight. So you're going to have to run, jog, bike, swim, or skip rope to develop sound cardiorespiratory conditioning. Each aerobic workout should last a minimum of 30 minutes and be performed at least four times per week.

The second component of physical fitness is muscular/skeletal conditioning. In the streets, the strong survive and the rest go to the morgue. To strengthen your bones and muscles to withstand the rigors of a real fight, your program must include progressive resistance (weight training) and calisthenics. You will also need a stretching program designed to loosen up every muscle group. You can't kick, punch, ground fight, or otherwise execute the necessary body mechanics if you're "tight" or inflexible. Stretching on a regular basis will also increase the muscles' range of motion, improve circulation, reduce the possibility of injury, and relieve daily stress.

The final component of physical fitness is proper body composition: simply, the ratio of fat to lean body tissue. Your diet and training regimen will affect your level or percentage of body fat significantly. A sensible and consistent exercise program accompanied by a healthy and balanced diet will facilitate proper body composition. Do not neglect this important aspect of physical fitness.

Weapon and Technique Mastery

You won't stand a chance against a vicious assailant if you don't master the weapons and tools of fighting. In CFA, we teach our students both armed and unarmed methods of combat. Unarmed fighting requires that you master a complete arsenal of natural body weapons and techniques. In conjunction, you must also learn the various stances, hand positioning, footwork, body mechanics, defensive structure, locks, chokes, and various holds. Keep in mind that something as simple as a basic punch will actually require hundreds of hours to perfect.

Range proficiency is another important aspect of weapon and technique mastery. Briefly, range proficiency is the ability to fight effectively in all three ranges of unarmed fighting. Although punching range tools are emphasized in CFA, kicking and grappling ranges cannot be neglected. Our kicking range tools consist of deceptive and powerful low-line kicks. Grappling range tools include head-butts, elbows, knees, foot stomps, biting, tearing, gouging, and crushing tactics.

Although CFA focuses on striking, we also teach our students a myriad of chokes, locks, and holds that can be used in a ground fight. While such grappling range submission techniques are not the most preferred methods of dealing with a ground fighting situation, they must be studied for the following six reasons: (1) level of force - many ground fighting situations do not justify the use of deadly force. In such instances, you must apply various non-lethal submission holds, (2) nature of the beast - in order to escape any choke, lock or hold, you must first know how to apply them yourself, (3) occupational requirement- some professional occupations (police, security, etc.) require that you possess a working knowledge of various submission techniques, (4) subduing a friend or relative - in many cases it is best to restrain and control a friend or relative with a submission hold instead of striking him with a natural body weapon, (5) anatomical orientation - practicing various chokes, locks and holds will help you develop a strong orientation of the human anatomy, and (6) refutation requirement - finally, if you are going to criticize the combative limitations of any submission hold, you better be sure that you can perform it yourself.

Contemporary Fighting Arts is more than a self defense system, its a one-of-a-kind martial arts style geared for real world self defense.

Defensive tools and skills are also taught. Our defensive structure is efficient, uncomplicated, and impenetrable. It provides the fighter maximum protection while allowing complete freedom of choice for acquiring offensive control. Our defensive structure is based on distance, parrying, blocking, evading, mobility, and stance structure.

Simplicity is always the key.

Students are also instructed in specific methods of armed fighting. For example, CFA provides instruction about firearms for personal and household protection. We provide specific guidelines for handgun purchasing, operation, nomenclature, proper caliber, shooting fundamentals, cleaning, and safe storage. Our firearm program also focuses on owner responsibility and the legal ramifications regarding the use of deadly force.

CFA's weapons program also consists of natural body weapons, knives and edged weapons, single and double stick, makeshift weaponry, the side-handle baton, and oleoresin capsicum (OC) spray.

Combat Attributes

Your offensive and defensive tools are useless unless they are used strategically. For any tool or technique to be effective in a real fight, it must be accompanied by specific attributes. Attributes are qualities that enhance a particular tool, technique, or maneuver. Some examples include speed, power, timing, coordination, accuracy, non-telegraphic movement, balance, and target orientation.

CFA also has a wide variety of training drills and methodologies designed to develop and sharpen these combat attributes. For example, our students learn to ground fight while blindfolded, spar with one arm tied down, and fight while handcuffed.

Reality is the key. For example, in class students participate in full-contact exercises against fully padded assailants, and real weapon disarms are rehearsed and analyzed in a variety of dangerous scenarios. Students also train with a large variety of equipment, including heavy bags, double-end bags, uppercut bags, pummel bags, focus mitts, striking shields, mirrors, rattan sticks, foam and plastic bats, kicking pads, knife drones, trigger-sensitive (mock) guns, boxing and digit gloves, full-body armor, and hundreds of different environmental props.

There are more than two hundred unique training methodologies used in Contemporary Fighting Arts. Each one is scientifically designed to prepare students for the hard-core realities of real world combat. There are also three specific training methodologies used to develop and sharpen the fundamental attributes and skills of armed and unarmed fighting, including proficiency training, conditioning training, and street training.

CFA has a several unique military combat training programs. Our mission is to provide today's modern soldier with the knowledge, skills and attitude necessary to survive a wide variety of real world combat scenarios. Our military program is designed to provide the modern soldier with the safest and most effective skills and tactics to control and decentralize armed and unarmed enemies.

Proficiency training can be used for both armed and unarmed skills. When conducted properly, proficiency training develops speed, power, accuracy, non-telegraphic movement, balance, and general psychomotor skill. The training objective is to sharpen one specific body weapon, maneuver, or technique at a time by executing it over and over for a prescribed number of repetitions. Each time the technique or maneuver is executed with "clean" form at various speeds. Movements are also performed with the eyes closed to develop a kinesthetic "feel" for the action. Proficiency training can be accomplished through the use of various types of equipment, including the heavy bag, double-end bag, focus mitts, training knives, real and mock pistols, striking shields, shin and knee guards, foam and plastic bats, mannequin heads, and so on.

Conditioning training develops endurance, fluidity, rhythm, distancing, timing, speed, footwork, and balance. In most cases, this type of training requires the student to deliver a variety of fighting combinations for three- or four-minute rounds separated by 30-second breaks. Like proficiency training, this type of training can also be performed at various speeds. A good workout consists of at least five rounds. Conditioning training can be performed on the bags with full-contact sparring gear, rubber training knives, focus mitts, kicking shields, and shin guards, or against imaginary assailants in shadow fighting.

Conditioning training is not necessarily limited to just three- or four-minute rounds. For example, CFA's ground fighting training can last as long as 30 minutes. The bottom line is that it all depends on what you are training for.

Street training is the final preparation for the real thing. Since many violent altercations are explosive, lasting an average of 20 seconds, you must prepare for this possible scenario. This means delivering explosive and powerful compound attacks with vicious intent for approximately 20 seconds, resting one minute, and then repeating the process.

Street training prepares you for the stress and immediate fatigue of a real fight. It also develops speed, power, explosiveness, target selection and recognition, timing, footwork, pacing, and breath control. You should practice this methodology in different lighting, on different terrains, and in different environmental settings. You can use different types of training equipment as well. For example, you can prepare yourself for multiple assailants by having your training partners attack you with focus mitts from a variety of angles, ranges, and target postures. For 20 seconds, go after them with vicious low-line kicks, powerful punches, and devastating strikes.

When all is said and done, the physical component creates a fighter who is physically fit and armed with a lethal arsenal of tools, techniques, and weapons that can be deployed with destructive results.

The Mental Component

The mental component of CFA focuses on the cerebral aspects of a fighter, developing killer instinct, strategic/tactical awareness, analysis and integration skills, philosophy, and cognitive skills.

The Killer Instinct

Deep within each of us is a cold and deadly primal power known as the "killer instinct." The killer instinct is a vicious combat mentality that surges to your consciousness and turns you into a fierce fighter who is free of fear, anger, and apprehension. If you want to survive the horrifying dynamics of real criminal violence, you must cultivate and utilize this instinctive killer mentality.

There are 14 characteristics of CFA's killer instinct. They are: (1) clear and lucid thinking, (2) heightened situational awareness, (3) adrenaline surge, (4) mobilized body, (5) psychomotor control, (6) absence of distraction, (7) tunnel vision, (8) fearless mind-set, (9) tactical implementation, (10) the lack of emotion, (11) breath control, (12) pseudospeciation, (13) viciousness, and (14) pain tolerance.

Visualization and crisis rehearsal are just two techniques used to develop, refine, and channel this extraordinary source of strength and energy so that it can be used to its full potential.

Strategic/Tactical Awareness

Strategy is the bedrock of preparedness. In CFA, there are three unique categories of strategic awareness that will diminish the likelihood of criminal victimization. They are criminal awareness, situational awareness, and self-awareness. When developed, these essential skills prepare you to assess a wide variety of threats instantaneously and accurately. Once you've made a proper threat assessment, you will be able to choose one of the following five self-defense options: comply, escape, de-escalate, assert, or fight back.

CFA also teaches students to assess a variety of other important factors, including the assailant's demeanor, intent, range, positioning and weapon capability, as well as such environmental issues as escape routes, barriers, terrain, and makeshift weaponry. In addition to assessment skills, CFA also teaches students how to enhance perception and observation skills.

Analysis and Integration Skills

The analytical process is intricately linked to understanding how to defend yourself in any threatening situation. If you want to be the best, every aspect of fighting and personal protection must be dissected. Every strategy, tactic, movement, and concept must be broken down to its atomic parts. The three planes (physical, mental, spiritual) of self-defense must be unified scientifically through arduous practice and constant exploration.

CFA's most advanced practitioners have sound insight and understanding of a wide range of sciences and disciplines. They include human anatomy, kinesiology, criminal justice, sociology, kinesics, proxemics, combat physics, emergency medicine, crisis management, histrionics, police and military science, the psychology of aggression, and the role of archetypes.

CFA's mental component focuses on the cognitive development of a fighter, including strategic/tactical awareness, analysis and integration, cognitive skills, the killer instinct, and philosophy.

Analytical exercises are also a regular part of CFA training. For example, we conduct problem-solving sessions involving particular assailants attacking in defined environments. We move hypothetical attackers through various ranges to provide insight into tactical solutions. We scrutinize different methods of attack for their general utility in combat. We also discuss the legal ramifications of self-defense on a frequent basis.

In addition to problem-solving sessions, students are slowly exposed to concepts of integration and modification. Oral and written examinations are given to measure intellectual accomplishment. Unlike traditional systems, CFA does not use colored belts or sashes to identify the student's level of proficiency.

Philosophy

Philosophical resolution is essential to a fighter's mental confidence and clarity. Anyone learning the art of war must find the ultimate answers to questions concerning the use of violence in defense of himself or others. To advance to the highest levels of combat awareness, you must find clear and lucid answers to such provocative questions as could you take the life of another, what are your fears, who are you, why are you interested in studying Contemporary Fighting Arts, why are you reading this book, and what is good and what is evil? If you haven't begun the quest to

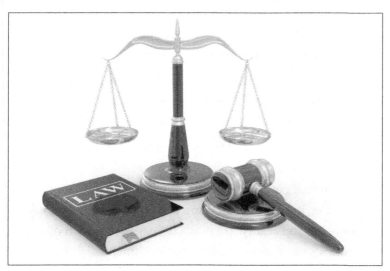

Developing a deadly capability to protect yourself carries tremendous moral and social responsibility. It also involves the risk of civil liability and criminal jeopardy. There is an interesting irony facing most martial artists or self-defense experts. The more highly trained, knowledgeable, and skilled you are in firearms, knives, unarmed combat tactics, martial arts, and other self-defense skills, the higher the standards of care you must follow when protecting yourself and others.

formulate these important questions and answers, then take a break. It's time to figure out just why you want to know the laws and rules of destruction.

Cognitive Combat Skills

Cognitive combat exercises are also important for improving one's fighting skills. CFA uses visualization and crisis rehearsal scenarios to improve general body mechanics, tools and techniques, and maneuvers, as well as tactic selection. Mental clarity, concentration, and emotional control are also developed to enhance one's ability to call upon the controlled killer instinct.

The Spiritual Component

There are many tough fighters out there. In fact, they reside in every town in every country. However, most are nothing more than vicious animals that lack self-mastery. And self-mastery is what separates the true warrior from the eternal novice.

I am not referring to religious precepts or beliefs when I speak of CFA's spiritual component. Unlike most martial arts, CFA does not merge religion into its spiritual aspect. Religion is a very personal and private matter and should never, be incorporated into any fighting system.

CFA's spiritual component is not something that is taught or studied. Rather, it is that which transcends the physical and mental aspects of being and reality. There is a deeper part of each of us that is a tremendous source of truth and accomplishment.

In CFA, the spiritual component is something that is slowly and progressively acquired. During the challenging quest of combat training, one begins to tap the higher qualities of human nature. Those elements of our being that inherently enable us to know right from wrong and good from evil. As we slowly develop this aspect of our total self, we begin to strengthen qualities profoundly important to the "truth." Such qualities are essential to your growth through the mastery of inner peace, the clarity of your "vision," and your recognition of universal truths.

While there are many dedicated individuals who are more than qualified to teach unique philosophical and spiritual components of ancient martial arts, you must realize that such forms of combat can get you killed in a real life self-defense encounter.

One of the goals of my system is to promote virtue and moral responsibility in people who have extreme capacities for physical and mental destructiveness. The spiritual component of fighting is truly the most difficult aspect of personal growth. Yet, unlike the physical component, where the practitioner's abilities will be limited to some degree by genetics and other natural factors, the spiritual component of combat offers unlimited potential for growth and development. In the final analysis, CFA's spiritual component poses the greatest challenges for the student. It is an open-ended plane of unlimited advancement.

Chapter 1
Knife Fighting Survival Concepts

Four Survival Concepts

Before jumping into the specific knife fighting techniques, it's important first to cover a few important concepts that will significantly enhance your safety and survival during a knife fight. They include the following:

- **Situational Awareness**
- **Threat Assessment**
- **Avoiding Excessive Force**
- **Controlling Fear**

Situational Awareness

Situational awareness is total alertness, presence, and focus on virtually everything in your immediate surroundings. You must train your senses to detect and assess the people, places, objects, and actions that can pose a danger to you. Do not think of situational awareness simply in terms of the five customary senses of sight, sound, smell, taste, and touch. In addition, the very real powers of instinct and intuition must also be developed and eventually relied upon.

Two vagrants congregating on the street corner or by your car, the stranger lingering at the mailboxes in your lobby, the delivery man at the door, a deserted parking lot, an alleyway near a familiar sidewalk, the stray dog ambling toward you in the park, a large limb hanging precariously from a tree . . . these are all obvious examples of persons, places, and objects that can pose a threat to you. Situational awareness need not - and should not - be limited to preconceived notions about obvious sources of danger.

Unfortunately, very few people have refined their situational awareness skills. The reasons are many. Some are in denial about the prevalence of criminal violence while others are too distracted

The 10 Best Knife Fighting Techniques

by life's everyday problems and pressures to pay attention to the hidden dangers that lurk around them. Whatever the reasons, poor awareness skills can get you into serious trouble and could cost you your life.

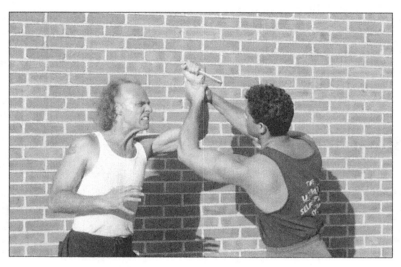

During a SHTF situation, situational awareness is total alertness, presence, and focus on virtually everything in your immediate surroundings. You must train your senses to detect and assess the people, places, objects, and actions that can pose a danger to you.

Situational awareness, in terms of threats posed by human attackers, begins with an understanding of criminal psychology. It is a common misconception that criminals are stupid and incompetent. Although many may be uneducated by traditional standards, they are not stupid. On the contrary, they can be shrewd, methodical, bold, and psychologically dominant. The especially dangerous ones are often expert observers of human behavior, capable of accurately assessing your body language, walk, talk, carriage, state of mind, and a variety of other indicators. They know what to look for and how to exploit it.

22

Criminals are also selective predators. Many rapists, for example, will test a victim by engaging her in idle conversation, following her, or invading her space in some preliminary and seemingly harmless manner. Carefully selected measures designed to evaluate fear, apprehension, and awareness are part of the attacker's overall strategy. Seasoned criminal aggressors are looking for easy strikes - what they call the "vic." Chronic brawlers, street punks, and muggers operate in the same basic manner. They look for the weak, timid, disoriented, and unaware victims.

As you develop situational awareness, you transmit a different kind of signal to the enemy's radar. Weakness and uncertainty are replaced by confidence and strength. Your carriage and movements change. You will be seen as assertive and purposeful. You are less likely to be perceived as an easy mark or a "vic," and your chances of being attacked will significantly diminish.

Situational awareness also diminishes the potency of the criminal's favorite weapon—surprise. Your ability to foresee and detect danger will diminish his ability to stalk you, or lie in wait in ambush zones. Ambush zones are strategic locations from which criminal assailants launch their attacks. Every day millions of Americans walk through numerous ambush zones and never even know it. Ambush zones are everywhere. They can be found and exploited in unfamiliar and familiar environments, even in your home, and in unpopulated and populated areas. An ambush zone can be set in a dark or poorly lit area as well as in a well-lit area. An ambush zone can be established in a variety of common places: under, behind, or around trees, utility boxes, shrubs, beds, corners, dumpsters, doorways, walls, tables, cars, trash cans, rooftops, bridges, ramps, mailboxes, etc. They are everywhere!

In addition to enhancing your ability to detect, avoid, and strategically neutralize ambush zones, situational awareness allows you to detect and avoid threats and dangers not necessarily predicated on the element of surprise. Some situations afford potential victims the luxury of actually seeing trouble coming. Nonetheless, it's remarkable how many people fail to heed obvious signs of danger because of poor awareness skills. They overlook the signals—belligerence, furtiveness, hostility, restlessness—so often manifested by criminal attackers. They neglect the opportunity to cross the street long before the shoulder-to-shoulder encounter with a pack of young toughs moving up the sidewalk. Once it's too late to avoid the confrontation, a whole new range of principles comes

Ambush zones are everywhere, how many do you see in this photo?

quickly into play. The best defense is a heightened level of situational awareness. You must learn to avoid situations that will require the use of physical force, and the highest form of self-defense is being smart enough to avoid a knife fight in the first place.

Situational awareness requires you to train all of your senses to detect and assess the people, places, objects, and actions that can pose a danger to you and your loved ones.

Situational Awareness Exercises

1. Detect five different ambush zones at your workplace and write them down. Don't pick the obvious ones. It's your life; learn to think like the criminal.

2. Detect five different ambush zones in front of your home. If you didn't find five, you didn't look hard enough.

3. Over the next ten days do not allow yourself to be taken by surprise—by anyone! Every time it happens, record the circumstances: who, what, when, how, where, and why.

4. When you watch television, go to the movies, look at pictures, or read books, note ambush zones that have not occurred to you in your other assessments. Note them in writing.

5. Visualize five different settings. They can be friendly and familiar like your backyard, or hostile and strange. Write down the things that you have mentally noted in these visualized settings.

Self Awareness

Self-awareness has been the subject of philosophers and mystics for centuries. Socrates said, "Know thyself." He believed self-knowledge to be essential to the attainment of true virtue.

Self-awareness is a critical component of knife fighting, but what does it mean to know yourself? Of course, you know your tastes and preferences, your desires, your occupation, and so forth. But do you know who you really are? What aspects of your self provoke violence and which, if any, would promote a proper reaction in defense against a threat of violence to you or others? Let's look at certain aspects important to self-protection and ask ourselves a few tough questions.

Physical Attributes

What are your physical strengths and weaknesses? Are you overweight or underweight? Is your body language and the manner in which you carry yourself more likely to provoke or deter a violent attack? Do you have any training in knife fighting? Are you fit or out of shape? Do you have the skill to disarm a knife-wielding attacker? Do you smoke or drink excessively? Are you skilled with firearms or edged weapons?

Mental Attributes

What are your mental strengths and weaknesses? Are you an optimist or pessimist? Can you summon up courage and confidence even when you are feeling fearful or insecure? How do you handle stress? Do you panic or frighten easily? Do you have any phobias? What are your fears? Do you think well on your feet?

Communication Skills

What are your strengths and weaknesses in expressing yourself with words? Are you likely to aggravate or diffuse a hostile situation? Are your words congruent with your tone of voice? Can you communicate adequately under stressful situations, or do you become nonplused?

Personality Traits

What type of person are you? Are you passive or aggressive? Are you opinionated and argumentative or open-minded and deliberative? Are you fiery, loud, and boisterous, or quiet, subdued, and calm? Are you quick to anger? Do you harbor grudges? Are there sensitive issues or remarks that may cause you to lose your temper?

Gender and Age

What are the different types of violent crimes that are directed toward you because of your sex? Women are much more likely than men to be raped or abused by their spouses. On the other hand, males are more apt than females to be victims of homicides. Is your age an open invitation for an attack? Children are more likely to be molested or kidnapped than adults, and older adults are weaker and more vulnerable to attack than middle-aged people.

Occupation

Does the nature of your occupation make you or your family vulnerable to different forms of criminal violence? Are you involved with the military or law enforcement? Are you a celebrity? Do you have diplomatic or political connections? Do you control large sums of money or valuable drugs? Does your political affiliation make you or your family a likely target for kidnapping and terrorism?

Income Level

What types of crime are directed toward you because of your income level? Are you wealthy, comfortable, or poor? Does your income level make you and your family vulnerable to kidnapping for ransom? Or does your financial situation force you and your family to live in poor neighborhoods that invite violent crime? Are you wealthy and flashy with outward evidence of this wealth?

Self-Awareness Exercises

The following questions were designed to start you thinking in the important process of self-awareness. Use them to form an overall personal profile of yourself. The goal is to recognize traits that provoke and/or prevent a violent attack.

1. Think of five physical and five mental weaknesses that would inhibit your survival in a knife fighting situation.

2. Recall a very stressful situation. How did you react? How did you feel? Were you angry? Did you lose control? Were you calm, notwithstanding the pressure?

3. Ask a close friend or your spouse to evaluate your communication skills in a variety of situations with other people. Are you open and receptive, rude or polite, emphatic and expressive, or reserved and withdrawn? Do not react defensively to the critique you receive, even if you don't agree.

4. Look into the mirror and conjure up the following mental and emotional states, carefully noting your facial expressions as they arise: anger, happiness, sadness, depression, surprise, and fear.

5. Go back to the preceding exercise and focus on anger. Pay close attention to your facial expressions and other physiological manifestations. What do you see?

6. Think of three forms of violent crime that you may be subject to because of your lifestyle.

7. Think of three forms of violent crime that you may be subject to because of your gender.

8. To gain a better understanding of yourself, complete the following four exercises. Be frank and truthful.

- Do you believe you could take the life of another human being if you had to?

- List four of your greatest fears.

- What steps might you take to eliminate or diminish those fears?

- Name three issues, topics, comments, or situations that would provoke you to lose your temper.

What is Threat Assessment?

We assess many different things every day. For example, we assess such divergent things as shopping values, the pros and cons of career moves, and different aspects of our relationships with others. The requisite skills for these assessments vary, depending on the elements involved. Skills for assessing the effect of fluctuating interest rates on the stock market are very different from those necessary to assess the effect of a volcano on global weather patterns. The analytical processes may be similar, but the knowledge and skills need to be encountered individually, and not arbitrarily.

Similarly, in the world of knife combat, threat assessment is the process of rapidly gathering and analyzing information, then accurately evaluating it in terms of threat and danger. In general, you can assess people, places, objects, and actions. In addition, assessment skills require sharp perception and keen observation. Your perception skills can be heightened, and your ability to observe can be enhanced.

Threat assessment is the process of rapidly gathering and analyzing information, then accurately evaluating it in terms of threat and danger.

We gather information through our sensory processes. You see a movement in the shadows of your backyard. You hear footsteps approaching from behind you in a dark parking lot. You smell cigarette smoke in what you thought was a deserted area. You feel a breeze coming up your stairwell when all the doors and windows are supposed to be shut. You taste the sickening metallic flavor of fear in your mouth.

These five senses can be sharpened through a variety of exercises designed to develop both raw detection and learned identification capabilities. For example, sit alone in your backyard for a given period of time and catalog the various things your five senses detect. Next, list the possible sources of the sensory data. With practice, you will make remarkable progress from being unable to detect a particular sound or smell to not only detecting it quickly and accurately but also identifying its source. This development increases as these exercises are performed in different types of settings. Imagine, for example, the things you would hear, see, and smell on a dark night in the middle of a suburban park, as opposed to what you would experience standing in a dark urban alley. Remember, you are only limited by your imagination.

Additionally, you can also heighten your ability to observe. Have you ever noticed how keenly you study people, buildings, streets, signs, animals, and various other everyday things when you travel to a strange city or to another country? Watch a dog in a new environment, with its nose in the air and ears perked in alertness. People and animals tend to observe more actively in strange or new environments. This practice reveals an old survival process at work. Conversely, we tend to become less observant in familiar settings. We let our guard down, so to speak. For example, how many times has your wife or girlfriend changed her hair, or your husband or boyfriend shaved his beard, and you simply didn't notice it?

Here's the good news: observational skills can be expanded with application of an intelligent program. In my Contemporary Fighting Arts (CFA) self-defense system, students are instructed to practice quickly, memorizing lines of verse in a hectic setting. The turmoil around them can work to strengthen their concentration. In some situations students will practice studying scenes on the streets, trying to spot the threat or potential danger. It might be a suspicious man lurking in an alleyway, a group of restless youths congregating at a street corner, or a figure in a second-story window cradling what might be a high-powered rifle. These are just a few exercises to sharpen your self-defense and observational skills. Military and intelligence agencies are experts in this area of training.

Even though the senses can be sharpened and the powers of observation enhanced, the ability to process information varies with the individual. Two average untrained people who witness the same event are likely to report it differently. This is referred to as "individual perception." In part, previous experiences can determine the manner in which an individual will react to stimuli. People of different ages, cultures, or occupational backgrounds may see the same event very differently. The actual physical processes involved in perception are much the same in every person. But it is the manner in which data is interpreted that determines what a person sees. When it comes to knife fighting, you must attempt to remove preconceived notions, assumptions, and biases that may lead to dangerously incorrect conclusions or oversights. These false reactions form actual blocks to your ability to grasp reality.

Choosing The Right Self-Defense Response

Accurate assessment is critical in knife fighting for two reasons. First, it is imperative that you choose the most appropriate tactical response. There are five possible tactical responses to any particular self-defense situation, listed in order of increasing level of resistance:

- **Comply**
- **Escape**
- **De-escalate**
- **Assert**
- **Fight Back**

Accurate assessment skills will help you choose the appropriate response for the situation.

Comply means to obey the assailant's commands. For example, if you are held at gun point (out of disarming range) for the purpose of robbery, there is nothing to do but comply. Take out your wallet, take off your watch, hand over your car keys, do what you are told. Comply.

Escape or Tactical Retreat means to flee from the threat or danger safely and rapidly. For example, if you are being held hostage and your captor is distracted long enough for you to escape safely, then do it.

De-Escalate means the art and science of diffusing a hostile individual. Not every confrontation warrants fighting back. Often you will be able to use de-escalation skills to talk someone out of a possible violent encounter. An intoxicated loudmouth may be just the type of guy you can settle down and lead away from a problem with effective de-escalation skills.

Assert means standing up for you and your rights. Through effective communication skills you can thwart a person's efforts to intimidate, dominate, and control you. For example, let's say you're working late at the office and your boss makes sexual advances toward you. Now is the time to confront him and be assertive. In a firm and confidant manner, you tell him that you're not interested and that you want him to stop his offensive actions immediately.

Fight Back means using various physical and psychological tactics and techniques to stun, incapacitate, cripple or kill your attacker(s). For example, you're trapped in a dead-end alley by a knife-wielding psychotic who appears determined to butcher you. Your only option is to fight back!

These are just a few of the many possible examples of the five tactical responses. Every self-defense situation is different, and, moreover, most situations can be fluid. A dangerous situation might present an escape option at one moment but quickly turn into a fight-back situation at the next. For example, let's say that you are kidnapped and your captor leaves a door unlocked, and in your effort to escape, you run into him on your way out. Obviously, that is the time to fight for your life.

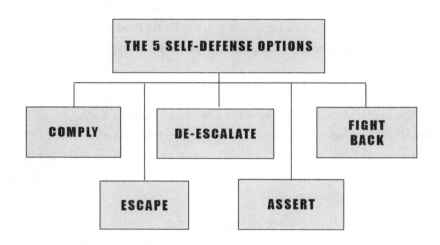

Avoiding Excessive Force

There is a second important reason why assessment skills are critical in knife fighting: the law. There is an interesting irony facing all law enforcement officers, self-defense, and martial art experts. The more highly trained, knowledgeable, and better you are in knives, combat tactics, martial arts, and other self-defense skills, the higher the standard of care you must observe when protecting yourself or others. If you act too quickly or use what someone might consider "excessive force" in neutralizing an assailant, you may end up being a defendant in a legal process.

America is the most violent society on earth. It is also the most litigious. Most people do not realize that developing a deadly capability to protect yourself carries a tremendous moral and social responsibility. It also involves the risk of civil liability and criminal jeopardy. If you blind or cripple a person, you'd better be prepared to justify this act in the eyes of the law. If you're not careful, you could spend the rest of your life supporting the person who meant to harm you - assuming, of course, that you can get a job once you get out of jail!

The two most popular questions students ask after they have had a little self-defense training are when can you use physical force, and how much physical force is justified? Well, there are no simple answers to these questions. Again, every self-defense situation is different. In one case, a side kick that dislocates an attacker's knee might be judged appropriate force. Change the facts a little and you have a civil battery suit and a criminal charge of aggravated assault. Killing a criminal attacker in one situation may be justified, but a seemingly similar case might result in a civil suit for wrongful death and a criminal charge of manslaughter or murder.

The basic principle is that you must never use force against another person unless it is justified. For civilians, force is broken down into two broad categories: lethal and nonlethal. Any time you use physical force against another person, you run the risk of having a civil suit filed against you. Anyone can hire a lawyer and file a suit for damages. Likewise, anyone can file a criminal complaint against you. Whether criminal charges will be brought against you depends upon the prosecutor or grand jury's views of the facts. No two cases are the same, so there are no easy answers.

I am not qualified to be offering you legal advice. Frankly, I know enough about the law not to make that mistake. However, I can tell you that if you are a highly trained self-defense expert, you will be held to a higher standard of behavior by a jury of your peers. Now there's a good one for you - a jury of your peers. If I ever have to be on trial, I hope that the jury will be comprised of twelve trained self-defense experts. But I won't hold my breath.

A particular troublesome angle to self-defense and legal liability is my first-strike principle (FSP). In many cases, jurors will decide self-defense issues on who struck whom first. That's not good news. My rule is: when faced with a harmful or deadly force situation, and when danger is imminent, then strike first, strike fast, and strike with authority. The problem arises because you may have a hard time justifying your approach in the antiseptic and safe environment of a courtroom many months later. Whenever my life has been in imminent danger, I always acted swiftly. Whether you adopt this approach is entirely up to you.

When to Use Assessment Skills

You should always be alert. Don't become complacent and comfortable. Never assume there is no danger! Learn to assess the situation promptly and accurately, reach a rational conclusion, and choose the appropriate tactical response. The only time you should forget about assessment is when you've been attacked by surprise. For example, a mugger lunges from behind a car, grabs you by the throat, and throws you to the ground. Then it's too late for assessment skills. You must act intuitively and immediately to neutralize him, or you're going to be a statistic. Remember, time is of the essence, and your reaction and reflex must take the place of assessment.

What to Assess

There are two broad factors to assess in any self-defense situation: the environment and the individual(s). Let's first look at the environment and its related factors.

The Environment

In any knife fighting situation you must strategically evaluate your environment, which is made up of your immediate surroundings. It can be a parking lot, your car, your bedroom, your office, an airport, a park, elevator, nightclub, movie theater, etc. There are four essential factors to consider when assessing your environment. They are escape routes, barriers, makeshift weapons, and terrain. Let's take a look at each one.

Escape routes. These are the various avenues or exits from a threatening situation. There is nothing cowardly about running away from a dangerous situation. The ultimate goal of a knife fight is to survive. Some possible escape routes are windows, doors, fire escapes, gates, escalators, fences, walls, bridges, and staircases. But be careful that your version of an escape route doesn't lead you into a worse situation.

Barriers. A barrier is any object that obstructs the attacker's path of attack. At the very least, barriers give you distance and some precious time, and they may give you some safety—at least temporarily. A barrier must have the structural integrity to perform the particular function you have assigned it. Barriers are everywhere and include such things as large desks, doors, automobiles, Dumpsters, large trees, fences, walls, heavy machinery, and large vending machines. The list is endless and depends on the situation, but it is a good idea to assess in advance any possible barriers when entering a potentially hostile or dangerous environment.

Makeshift weapons. These are common, everyday objects that can be converted into offensive and defensive weapons. Like a barrier, a makeshift weapon must be appropriate to the function you have assigned to it. You won't be able to knock someone out with a car antennae, but you could whip it across their eyes and temporarily blind them. Whereas you could knock someone unconscious with a good heavy flashlight but you could not use it to shield yourself from a knife attack.

Makeshift weapons can be broken down into four types: striking, distracting, shielding, and cutting weapons.

Striking makeshift weapons, as the name implies, are objects that can be used to strike an assailant. Examples include heavy flashlights, baseball bats, bottles, beer mugs, text books, binoculars, small lamps, hammers, pool cues, canes, umbrellas, vases, walking sticks, crowbars, light dumbbells, barstools, chairs, etc.

Distracting makeshift weapons are objects that can be thrown at the attacker(s) to temporarily distract him. Depending on the size of the object, a distraction weapon can be thrown into an assailant's face, body, or legs. They include car keys, glass bottles, rolled-up newspaper or magazine, text books, dirt, gravel, sand, hot liquids, spare change, ashtrays, paperweights, wallets, purses, and briefcases. Trash cans, chairs, and bicycles can also be kicked or slammed into an assailant's legs.

Shielding makeshift weapons are objects that temporarily shield you from the assailant's punch, kick, or strike. In some cases, shielding weapons can also be used to protect against knife and bludgeon attacks. Examples of shielding weapons include: trash can lids, briefcases, luggage bags, doors, sofa cushions, thick pillows, ironing boards, hubcaps, food trays, lawn chairs, small tables, backpack, etc.

Cutting makeshift weapons are objects that can be used to cut the assailant by either stabbing or slashing him. Examples include all kitchen cutlery, forks, screwdrivers, broken bottles, broken glass, scissors, car keys, pitch forks, ice scrapers, letter openers, pens, sharp pencils, razor blades, etc. Obviously there is some overlap between the various categories of make-shift weapons. For example, a briefcase can be thrown into an attacker's face for distraction, used to shield against a knife attack, or slammed into an assailant's temple to knock him out.

Terrain. This is a critical environmental factor. What are the strategic implications of the terrain that you are standing on? Will the surface area interfere with your ability to defend against an assailant? Is the terrain wet or dry, mobile or stationary? Obviously, if you are standing on ice, you will be restricted in your efforts to quickly escape or attempt kicking techniques. If the surface is shaky, like a suspension bridge, for example, you may be required to avoid kicking your assailant and instead fight back with hand techniques.

The Individual(s)

Obviously, in a potentially dangerous situation, you need to assess the source of the threat. Who is posing the possible danger? Is it someone you know or is he a complete stranger? Is it one person or two or more? What are his or her intentions in confronting you? Pay attention to all available clues, particularly verbal and nonverbal indicators. Let all five of your senses go to work to absorb the necessary information. Also don't forget to listen to what your gut instincts are telling you about the threatening person(s). There are five essential factors to consider when assessing a threatening individual: demeanor, intent, range, positioning, and weapon capability.

Demeanor. In the broadest terms we are talking about the individual's outward behavior. Watch for clues and cues. Is he shaking, or is he calm and calculated? Are his shoulders hunched or relaxed? Are his hands clenched? Is his neck taut? Are his teeth clenched? Is he breathing hard? Does he seem angry or frustrated, or confused and scared? Does he seem high on drugs? Is he mentally ill or simply intoxicated? What is he saying? How is he saying it? Is his speech slurred? What is his tone of voice? Is he talking rapidly or methodically? Is he cursing and angry? All of these verbal and nonverbal cues are essential in assessing the individual's overall demeanor and thus adjusting your tactical response accordingly.

Intent. Once you've got a good read on the assailant's demeanor, you're in a much better position to assess his or her intent. In other words, just what is this person's purpose in confronting you? Does he intend to rob you? Is he seeking retribution for something you have done? Or is he simply looking to pick a fight with you? Determining the individual's intent is perhaps the most important assessment factor, but it can also be the most difficult. Moreover, when it comes to criminal intent, things can change pretty quickly. For example, an intent to rob can quickly turn into an intent to rape. In any event, the appropriate tactical response is highly dependent upon a correct assessment of intent.

Range. Range is the spatial relationship between you and the assailant(s) in terms of distance. In self-defense there are three possible distances from which your assailant can launch an attack: Kicking range, Punching range, and Grappling range. Kicking range is the furthest range from which the attacker can kick you, lunge at you with or without a weapon, or strike you with a bludgeon. Punching range is the midrange from which the attacker can strike you with his hands, grab or push you, cut you with a knife, or strike you with a bludgeon. Grappling range is the closest range, from which the assailant can wrestle, grab, push, or choke you, and cut you with an edged weapon. When assessing a threatening individual, you'll need to recognize the strategic implications of his range. For example, how close is he from launching a punch? Is he at a distance from which he could kick you? Is he in a range that allows him to grab hold of you, take you to the ground, or cut you with an edged weapon? Is he moving through the ranges of unarmed combat? If so, how fast? Does he continue to move forward when you step back?

Positioning. This is the spatial relationship of the assailant(s) to you in terms of threat, escape, and target selection. Are you surrounded by multiple assailants or only one? Is he standing squarely or sideways, above or below you? What anatomical targets does the assailant present you with? Is he blocking the door or any other avenue of escape? Is his back to the light source? Is he close to your only makeshift weapon? You must answer these questions before choosing a tactical strategy appropriate to the situation.

Weapon capability. Is your assailant armed or unarmed? If he is carrying a weapon, what type is it? Does he have a delivery method for the particular weapon? Is he armed with more than one weapon? Sometimes it is easy to determine if someone is armed. For example, you see a knife sheath on his belt. At other times your assessment skills need to be more advanced. For example, is the person wearing a jacket when it is too hot for a jacket? Could it be to conceal a gun at the waist? Is the person patting his chest? When scanning the person, can you see his hands and all his fingertips? Is one hand behind him or in his pockets? Could he be palming a knife or some other edged weapon? Are his arms crossed? Does he seem to be reaching for something? Does he seem suspiciously rooted to a particular spot? Is his body language incongruous with his verbal cues you are reading? The CFA rule: When you're not certain, always assume your assailant is armed with a weapon.

Controlling Fear

To the untrained person, any kind of violent encounter (especially a knife fight) will result in some level of fear. Fear is a strong and unpleasant emotional reaction to a real or perceived threat. If uncontrolled, fear leads to panic. Then it's too late to adequately protect yourself.

The Three Levels of Fear

To prevent the negative effects of fear during a knife fight, you need to understand its levels and dynamics. For analysis, I have categorized fear into three different levels, listed in order of intensity:

- Fright (quick or sudden fear)
- Panic (overpowering fear)
- Terror (crippling or immobilizing fear)

While these three levels of fear vary in degrees of stress, they all have one common root response: the fight-or-flight response.

What is The Fight-or-Flight Response?

Whenever a person, or any animal for that matter, feels threatened or frightened, certain physiological changes occur. They start in the brain when the hypothalamus sends strong impulses to the pituitary gland, causing it to release a hormone (ACTH) that stimulates the adrenal glands to release other hormones into the bloodstream.

Ultimately every nerve and muscle is involved. This adrenaline will cause an increased heart rate with a corresponding increase in respiration and blood pressure. Your muscles will tense up, you will start to sweat, and your mouth will go dry. In addition, your digestive system will shut down to allow a better supply of blood to the muscles. Your hair will stand on end (piloerection). Your pupils will enlarge so that your vision can improve. Your hand and limbs will also begin to tremble. Once these biochemical mechanisms and processes are fully engaged - and it takes only nanoseconds - your body will be in the fight-or-flight mode.

For most people, the fight-or-flight response has a debilitating effect. They panic or freeze up, and fear then becomes a powerful weapon of the attacker. By paralyzing you with fear, his job is easier. Therefore, it is critically important that you learn to control the fight-or-flight response to make it work for you and not against you in a knife fight.

First, accept the fact that the fight-or-flight response is a natural human response. In fact, it's one of Mother Nature's best ways of helping you survive a dangerous situation. You've got to take advantage of this assistance by using the energy of the adrenaline surge to augment your counterattack and awaken your killer instinct. The killer instinct burns on the fuel of adrenaline and can be a vicious and lethal source of energy. Properly channeled, this destructiveness will exceed that of your assailant, and you will overwhelm him.

Second, harness the fight-or-flight response by preparing yourself thoroughly for the danger that may one day confront you. Developing the psychological and physical skills of your self-defense weapon will lead to a personal self-confidence. In turn, this confidence leads to an inner calm. Inner calm is the environment necessary to the killer instinct, and the killer instinct will drink adrenaline like a race horse drinks water.

Your preparation involves learning the physical skills, techniques, and tactics required to use your weapon effectively. The only way to achieve these skills and techniques is with a qualified reality based self-defense instructor and realistic training (e.g., simulated assaults with tough physical contact).

This type of physical training leads to psychological preparedness. Once you begin to understand what a physical confrontation consists of, you can expand your training to visualize such confrontations and the necessary control over the fight-or-flight syndrome.

You must continue to develop this keen sense of self-awareness to be psychologically prepared for a violent confrontation. Never stop assessing your state of mind and reactions to different stressful situations. For example, the next time you are startled by something, pay close attention. What was it that startled you and why? Did you freeze up? What did you see? What did you hear? Were you trembling and breathing heavily? Was your mind clear or distracted? Exactly what were you thinking about? How much detail can you remember? Did you make any tactical errors in your responses? These are only a few of the questions you should answer over and over again as you go through the process of preparing yourself psychologically.

Another method of psychological preparation is written analysis. For example, write down five different hypothetical scenarios (i.e., carjacking, robbery, knife fight, etc.) that truly frighten you. These scenarios could take place anywhere (home, workplace, street, hiking trail, parking lot). Be specific with your details. Make certain to include the following relevant factors:

- **Time of day**

- **Environment**

- **Attacker's description**

- **Number of attackers**

- **Type of crime**

- **Assailant's intent**

- **Type of physical attack/assault**

- **Type of weapon**

- **Your immediate physical condition at time of attack**

- **Any other relevant factors to your scenario**

Once you've completed these scenarios, have your instructor identify the specific factors that elicit reasonable fear and then adjust your knife fighting training to meet your concerns.

In the interim, if you find yourself in a dangerous situation and cannot control your fight-or-flight response and you become overwhelmed with panic, quickly convert your fear into raw, vicious anger. That's right: get mad! Some low-life thug is about to injure or kill you or some loved one. Tear him apart. Relying purely on anger is not the best way of defending yourself, but your raw anger can still be a powerful emotion that can be used in your favor.

Pictured here, a diagram of the fight-or-flight response.

Possible Physiological Responses To Fear

- Enlarged pupils
- Dry mouth
- Trembling hands
- Cold, clammy hands
- Increased heart rate
- Shutdown of digestive system
- Tense muscles
- Sudden adrenaline surge
- Hair stands on end
- Enhanced alertness

How To Control Your Fear in a Knife Fight

Here are a few suggestions that will help you control the deleterious effects of fear:

- Learn the necessary skills and tactics of knife fighting.
- Be confident and competent with your weapon skills.
- Regularly practice knife fighting rehearsal (visualization) scenarios.
- Understand and accept the physiological responses to the fight-or-flight response.
- Learn how to tap and control your killer instinct.
- Evaluate your past responses to dangerous or threatening situations.
- Learn the differences between "perceptual danger" and "reasonable danger."
- Always believe in your knife fighting skills and abilities.

- Always trust your instincts and judgments.

- Develop accurate threat assessment skills.

- Adopt the will to survive.

- Always strive to be physically fit.

- Maintain a high degree of situational awareness at all times.

- Regularly practice assault scenarios with a spouse, friend, training partner, etc.

- Always keep a positive mental attitude.

Chapter Two
The 10 Best Knife Fighting Techniques

Avoid it at all costs!

I would be remiss if I did not start this chapter by stating that a knife fighting encounter is a desperate situation that should only be undertaken when all other means of avoiding the situation have been thoroughly exhausted.

Knife fighting is deadly and should be avoided at all costs. If you have the chance to run and escape during the course of a knife fight, do it immediately!

Also, never use a knife to threaten someone. A knife is a tool of destruction that is intended to injure or kill, not intimidate. Never pull a knife unless you're legally and morally justified to use it. A knife should only be displayed when you have no other choice but to cut your adversary to pieces. Period!

Buy a good blade

Before delving into the techniques and strategies of knife fighting, I want you to be aware that if you are going to carry a knife for self-defense, you must assume the legal and social responsibilities that go along with it.

Also, before you purchase a knife, check your state and local laws. In some states, certain knives are prohibited altogether. If you are going to carry a knife, make certain that you do so in a manner consistent with applicable laws.

Having said that, here a few important points to consider when purchasing a knife for knife fighting:

1. Make certain the knife fits comfortably in both your right and left hands.

2. Choose a knife that is designed for slashing as well as stabbing movements.

3. Get a knife that has a partially serrated edge. A serration is simply a sharpened recessed curve along the edge of the blade. Serrations act like teeth that will saw through tough clothing (especially leather). The serrations should also be located on the lower portion of the blade.

4. Choose a blade that is sharp and large enough to penetrate the assailant's vital arteries and organs.

5. Choose a knife that is light enough for you to manipulate easily and quickly.

6. Use either a lock blade or fixed blade made of high-carbon stainless steel.

7. If you are in the market for a fixed blade, try to purchase a knife that has a slight hand guard, which will prevent your hand from slipping onto the blade when you thrust it.

8. Avoid using a knife that has a wood or metal grip. Wood and metal grips provide poor gripping, especially when your hands are wet. Rubberized "sure grips" are essential for edged-weapon combat. Remember, puncture wounds will make your blade and grip bloody and slippery.

9. Avoid using spring blades (i.e., switchblades, stilettos) in a knife fight. They are inherently dangerous for the following reasons: (a) the internal spring can malfunction, (b) the structural integrity of the knife is usually poor, (c) the hand grips are usually too thin and often slippery, and (d) they look menacing and have a criminal stigma attached to them. Remember, if you are later taken to court, the jury will look unfavorably at you, even though you may have been justified in killing your adversary.

10. Avoid using pocket knives (e.g., Swiss Army pocket knives, Old Timer pocket knives, etc.) for knife fighting. Folding

blades are not designed for knife combat, which requires aggressive cutting and slashing movements. In most cases, when you are using a folding knife in a self-defense situation, the blade will fold and close on your fingers when you make contact with your target.

If you are going to use a tactical folding knife, be certain it has a solid locking mechanism. Lock blades stay locked open, preventing an accidental closure on your fingers or hand.

Folding pocket knives are not designed for knife combat, which requires aggressive cutting and slashing movements. Here's a good example of what you should never use in a knife fight.

The 10 Best Knife Fighting Techniques

In this chapter, I'm going to teach you some of my best knife fighting techniques. Keep in mind that every knife fight will be different and not every tactical tactic or technique is going to be ideal for your particular circumstance. It will be up to you to decide which one best suits your situation. Remember to always use your best judgment and never use any weapon against another person unless it's morally and legally justified in the eyes of the law.

1. Master the knife grips

One of the foundational elements of knife fighting is the grip. When I say, "grip," I am referring to how the knife is held and manipulated in the hand during a knife fight. When it comes to tactical knife combat, the grip should accomplish the following three objectives.

1. **Provides positive weapon retention** – The ability to retain your knife in the heat of battle is vital. This is especially important when your hands are sweaty or covered with the criminal's blood. Remember, never pick up a knife unless you are confident that you can maintain complete control of it. In Contemporary Fighting Arts, we have a saying, "Lose your weapon and you lose your life."

2. **Permits effective use and manipulation** – The ability to move and manipulate your blade goes without saying. The knife is a multi-directional weapon designed to change angles of attack in a split second.

3. **Helps manage "impact shock"** – If your blade hits bone (which is likely) you better have a grip that will manage the impact shock. Remember, cutting the air with your knife is nothing like making hard contact with flesh and bone.

When gripping your knife, always make certain that the cutting edge faces your assailant. I know this may seem obvious but would be amazed how many people make this mistake. Also, be very careful not to wrap your fingers too tightly around the handle. This can be dangerous for the following reasons:

1. It restricts wrist mobility.
2. It reduces your slashing and stabbing speed.
3. It weakens your forearm muscles.
4. It creates greater target exposure by forcing your veins to protrude from your hands and forearms.

In knife fighting, the two primary knife grips that you must master are as follows: (1) hammer grip (2) ice-pick grip.

Hammer Grip

Pictured here, the hammer grip which can be used for both slashing and stabbing techniques.

The hammer grip is the exact type of grip you would use if you were holding an actual hammer. Hence, the name - hammer grip.

Generally, when performing the hammer grip, the exposed area of the blade will be seen above your thumb line. The hammer grip can be used for both slashing and stabbing techniques.

Ice-Pick Grip

Next, is the ice pick grip. As you can imagine, this grip is similar to holding an ice pick in your hand. Generally, the exposed area of the blade will be seen below your pinky finger.

Like the hammer grip, the ice pick grip can also be used for both slashing and stabbing movements. However, sufficient wrist flexibility is required to perform many ice pick slashing movements. So, if you do have *tight* wrists, you might want to practice slashing movements with the ice pick grip until your wrists loosen up.

Pictured here, the ice pick grip which can be used for both slashing and stabbing techniques.

The ice pick grip is not just limited to knife fighting. It has numerous weapon applications, including the tactical pen.

When using the ice pick grip, don't make the novice mistake of holding the knife with the cutting edge facing away from the adversary.

2. Master the knife fighting stance

Surviving a vicious knife fight demands that you master a tactical knife fighting stance. The knife fighting stance that I am going to teach you provides maximal mobility, minimal target exposure, and facilitate immediate counter cutting ability. Here is an overview of the key points to a good knife fighting stance.

1. Keep your knees slightly bent and flexible, your feet a shoulder-width apart, and your weight equally distributed on each leg. This will permit quick footwork that is so vital for effective knife fighting. Angle your body (internal organs) approximately forty-five degrees from your assailant.

2. Deeply crouch your body, with your shoulders and stomach sunk inward.

3. Keep your head and face back and away from random slashes or stabs.

4. Place your guard hand (the one that is not holding the knife) in the center of your body.

5. Clench your fist of your guard hand and place it directly under your nose.

6. Keep your fist, forearms, and elbows directly in front of your centerline. This hand and arm configuration is critical.

7. Hold your knife in your front hand. This knife forward stance is critical because it brings your closest weapon (your knife) to the assailant's closest targets. In the majority of cases, a lead hand knife fighter will have a significant advantage over a rear hand knife fighter.

The Knife Fighting Stance

KNIFE IN FRONT HAND

SHOULDERS SLIGHTLY HUNCHED

STOMACH SUNK IN

REAR ARM HELD IN CENTER OF BODY

ELBOWS TUCKED IN

KNEES BENT

FEET PARALLEL

FEET SHOULDER-WIDTH APART

3. Knife fighting range proficiency

Knife fighting is fluid and dynamic and will often force you and your adversary to move in and out of ranges of engagement. In order to survive a knife fight, you will have to be proficient in all three ranges of knife combat. They include long, intermediate, and close-quarter distances. Let's start by taking a look at the long range of knife fighting.

Long range

This is the farthest distance of knife fighting where you can only reach and cut your opponent's hand or wrist flexor. The hammer grip is ideal for this range of combat.

The long range of knife fighting.

Intermediate range

Next, we have the intermediate range of knife fighting. At this distance you are close enough to cut the mid to upper portion of the opponent's arm (from his wrist flexor to his biceps). The hammer grip is still the most preferred grip for this distance of engagement.

Pictured here, the intermediate range of knife fighting.

Close Quarter range

At this distance, you are close enough to stab the opponent's body with the ice pick grip. Other secondary close-quarter combat techniques can also be applied (i.e., head butt, biting tactics, elbow strikes, etc).

Close-quarter knife fighting can also take place on the ground. Keep in mind that ground fighting with edged weapons is a treacherous task reserved for only the most skilled knife fighter.

The close-quarter range of knife combat.

4. Master footwork and mobility

Footwork and mobility are often the most overlooked aspect of knife fighting. Mobility is important for the following reasons:

1. It allows you to quickly move in and out of the range from various slashes and stabs.

2. It makes you a more evasive target, and in some cases it helps minimize your assailant's complete blade penetration.

3. Solid footwork permits you to change your direction of movement quickly and efficiently.

4. It improves your general reaction time.

5. It allows you to recover quickly from a committed movement.

I define mobility as the ability to move your body quickly and freely, which is accomplished through basic footwork. The safest footwork involves quick, economical steps performed on the balls of your feet, while you remain relaxed and balanced. Keep in mind that balance is your most important consideration.

Basic footwork can be used for both offensive and defensive purposes, and it is structured around four general directions: forward, backward, right, and left.

However, always remember this footwork rule of thumb: *Always move the foot closest to the direction you want to go first, and let the other foot follow an equal distance.* This prevents cross-stepping, which can cost you your life in a knife fight.

Basic Footwork Movements

1. Moving forward (advance) - from your knife fighting stance, first move your front foot forward (approximately 12 inches) and then move your rear foot an equal distance.

The 10 Best Knife Fighting Techniques

2. Moving backward (retreat) - from your knife fighting stance, first move your rear foot backward (approximately 12 inches) and then move your front foot an equal distance.

3. Moving right (sidestep right) - from your knife fighting stance, first move your right foot to the right (approximately 12 inches) and then move your left foot an equal distance.

4. Moving left (sidestep left) - from your knife fighting stance, first move your left foot to the left (approximately 12 inches) and then move your right foot an equal distance.

Practice these four movements for 10 to 15 minutes a day in front of a full-length mirror. In a couple weeks, your footwork should be quick, balanced, and natural.

Circling Right and Left

Strategic circling is an advanced form of footwork where you will use your front leg as a pivot point. This type of movement can also be used defensively to evade an attack or to counter cut the opponent from various strategic angles. Strategic circling can be performed from either a left or right stance.

- **Circling left (from a left stance)** - this means you'll be moving your body around the opponent in a clockwise direction. From a left stance, step 8 to 12 inches to the left with your left foot, then use your left leg as a pivot point and wheel your entire rear leg to the left until the correct stance and positioning is acquired.

- **Circling right (from a right stance)** - from a right stance, step 8 to 12 inches to the right with your right foot, then use your right leg as a pivot point and wheel your entire rear leg to the right until the correct stance and positioning is acquired.

5. Allow an avenue of escape

If you have the chance to run and escape during a knife fight, do it *immediately*! Quickly try to scan your environment for possible escape routes.

Look for doors, windows, stairwells, or other avenues of safe escape. Under no circumstances should you engage in a knife fight unless it is absolutely necessary. Don't let your ego or pride trap you into believing that it's cowardly to run from a knife fight. However, if you attempt to outrun your adversary, be certain that you have the athletic ability to really move - and don't offer him target opportunities in your flight.

Also, if your situation permits, *allow your assailant an avenue of escape*. Many people will choose to run once they catch the sight of their own blood. Avoid making the tragic mistake of forcing your assailant into a corner.

Something as simple as an avenue of escape can make all the difference between life and death for both you and your adversary.

6. Keep your knife in your front hand and close to your body

When knife fighting, hold your knife in your front hand. This knife-forward stance is critical for the following reasons:

1. It brings your closest weapon (your knife) to the assailant's closest targets.

2. The unprotected (or unarmed) side of your body is kept back and away from your assailant's stabs and slashes. Generally, a lead-hand knife fighter will have a tactical advantage over a rear-hand knife fighter.

Also, if you ever have the option or luxury of assuming a knife fighting stance, try to position your stronger and more coordinated side forward. For example, if you are right-handed, your right side is generally your stronger and more coordinated side. This strong-side stance is important for knife combat because it maximizes the speed, power, dexterity, and accuracy of your blade movement.

Finally, avoid overextending your knife hand. This is dangerous for the following reasons:

1. It inhibits your balance.

2. It leaves you vulnerable to attack.

3. It significantly reduces your ability to attack your assailant.

When holding your knife, keep it in your front hand and hold it close to your body. Keep your rear hand in with your elbow close to your body while keeping the belly of your forearm and palm facing your chest. This will keep the vulnerable flexors and blood vessels of your "secondary hand" away from random slashes from your assailant. The only time your knife should be away from your body is when you are executing an attack.

Knife fighting with the knife in your rear hand is dangerous for a number of reasons. Always keep your knife in your front hand.

Forget what you have seen in the movies, always keep your knife close to your body at all times.

7. Master the slash and stab

There are several ways to cut your adversary during a knife fight. Some are excellent and some are terrible. For simplicity sake, I will teach you two of the most important cuts you should master. They are the slash and the stab.

The Slash

A slash is one of the two best ways you can cut the adversary with a knife. Essentially, the *slash* is a quick, tight sweeping stroke made with the edge of the knife. The slash can be delivered in all the ranges of knife combat. Compared to stabs, slashing usually creates a larger surface area wound, so expect things to get bloody very fast!

Whenever executing slashing cuts, avoid wide and long arcing movements. Always keep your "slashing arc" tight and quick. Never lock your elbow when delivering any type of slashing motion. Exaggerated slashing movements are the true mark of a novice and it opens up a fighter to numerous vulnerabilities. Some include: possible elbow dislocation, reduced cutting power and speed, telegraphic movement, and extreme target exposure.

Finally, slashing movements are best delivered to the assailant's arms, eyes, neck, and knee region. Avoid slashing your assailant's torso, which is best suited for thrusts and stabs.

The Stab

A stab is a quick and forceful thrust made with the tip of the knife. Stabbing motions puncture body tissue and are more likely to be fatal because it produces severe internal damage and bleeding. Unlike the slash, the stab can only be utilized in the intermediate and close quarter ranges of knife combat. Never over commit your stab, you will most likely lose your balance and expose vital targets to the assailant.

Compared to stabs, slashing usually creates a larger surface area wound, so expect things to get bloody very fast.

When slashing at your adversary, be certain to make contact with the bottom portion of the blade first and then pull the rest of the blade through the target. This will maximize the size of the wound.

8. Exploit knife wound reaction dynamics

In my book, *Maximum Damage: Hidden Secrets Behind Brutal Fighting Combinations*, I define *probable reaction dynamics* (PRD) as the opponent's anticipated movements or actions that occur in both armed and unarmed combat. Probable reaction dynamics will always be the result or residual of your initial cut with a knife.

The most basic example of probable reaction dynamics during a knife fight can be illustrated by the following scenario. For example, your adversary attempts to cut you and you immediately counter cut him with a deep slash to the inside of his forearm. When your blade comes in contact with its target, your opponent will exhibit one of several "possible" physical or psychological reactions to your cut. These responses might include:

- The opponent reflexively retracts his injured arm.
- The opponent grabs or covers his wound.
- The opponent frantically looks for an escape route.
- The opponent continually looks at his injured arm.
- The opponent goes into shock.

Knowledge of your assailant's probable reaction dynamics is vital during a knife fight. In fact, you must be mindful of the possible reaction dynamics to every possible angle of attack with your knife. This is what I refer to as "reaction dynamic awareness" and I can assure you this is not such an easy task. However, with proper training and analysis, it can be developed.

Regardless of your knife fighting style, understanding and ultimately mastering reaction dynamic awareness will give you a tremendous advantage in a fight by maximizing the effectiveness, efficiency, and safety of your knife fighting skills.

Probable Reaction Dynamic Exercise

Write down the different probable reaction dynamics to the following knife wounds. Don't forget to include both offensive and defensive reactions.

A slash to the inside forearm

1.

2.

3.

4.

5.

A slash to the triceps

1.

2.

3.

4.

5.

A slash to the inner thigh (femoral artery)

1.

2.

3.

4.

5.

A slash to the back of the knee

1.

2.

3.

4.

5.

A stab under the armpit

1.

2.

3.

4.

5.

A stab to the groin

1.

2.

3.

4.

5.

9. Use your secondary hand

As I stated earlier, a good knife fighter will use everything he or she has at their disposal, including your free hand (the one that's not holding the knife) or what I like to call the *secondary hand*. Your secondary hand plays a vital role during a knife fight and it serves a few important functions including:

1. Checking, redirecting and controlling your opponent's limbs during the knife fight.

2. Blocking and parrying oncoming attacks.

Therefore, must also learn to practice quick slashing and stabbing movements with your secondary hand closely trailing your blade. This can be practiced and refined in front of a full-length mirror.

In this photo, Franco (left) uses his secondary hand to temporarily control his assailant's weapon hand.

10. Use your natural body weapons

Too many people assume that mere possession of a knife will guarantee their survival during an emergency self-defense situation. This assumption forms the popular fallacy of *dependency* - the sole reliance on the particular weapon for personal protection. While a knife is an essential tool during a knife fight, no single weapon is the definitive answer by itself. You must use everything at your disposal to ensure your survival.

Having said that, knife fighting is not just about using only your knife. Never forget that you have numerous secondary weapons or what I call *natural body weapons* at your immediate disposal.

Natural body weapons when knife fighting

If you want to be fully prepared for a possible knife fight, you must also have a working knowledge of your natural body weapons. Body weapons are simply the various parts of your body that can be used as weapons to neutralize your adversary.

You have fourteen natural body weapons at your disposal. They are easy to learn and, when properly executed, have the potential to disable, cripple, and even kill an attacker. They include the head, teeth, voice, elbows, fists, palms, fingers and nails, edge of hand, web of the hand, knees, shins, dorsum of the foot, heel of foot, and ball of foot. Let's take a look at each one.

Head

When you are knife fighting in close quarters, your head can be used for butting your assailant's nose. Head butts are ideal when a strong attacker has placed you in a hold where your arms are pinned against your sides.

Teeth

The teeth can be used for biting anything on the assailant's body (nose, ears, throat, fingers, etc.). It is important, however, for you to muster the mental determination to bite deep and hard into the assailant's flesh and shake your head vigorously, much like a vicious dog killing his enemy. While this may seem primitive and barbaric, it is essential to your survival.

Although a bite is extremely painful, it also transmits a strong psychological message to your assailant. It lets him know that you, too, can be vicious and are willing to do anything to survive the encounter.

Warning: There is one important concern to biting tactics: you run the risk of contracting AIDS if your attacker is infected and you draw blood while biting him.

Voice

Your voice is also a powerful weapon during a knife fight. When trained properly it can distract and startle your assailant, causing him to freeze temporarily.

Using your voice as a weapon

The voice can be a powerful weapon. When knife fighting, the yell is a natural manifestation of the voice. The yell was probably part of earliest man's expressions. He undoubtedly used the yell in his life-and-death battles long before he learned the most basic forms of spoken language. The North American Indians were proficient in using the yell to strike fear in their enemies.

Yelling actually serves a strategic purpose in self-defense. Yelling while fighting back can distract, startle, and temporarily paralyze your assailant. It can cause him to freeze in his tracks, allowing you that split second advantage to deliver the first debilitating strike and thus to gain offensive control.

Yelling can also be used to psyche out the criminal. Imagine this situation: one minute you're talking calmly to a threatening aggressor and the next you are suddenly emitting a blood-curdling yell and striking him. This dramatic reversal can throw an assailant into a psychological tailspin.

Yelling also synchronizes your state of mind with the physical process taking place. It is the catalyst that sets off the killer instinct. It is the primal expression that harbors the killer instinct. In addition, yelling actually may draw attention to your emergency situation. In many cases, muggers, rapists, and street punks will abort their attacks and run to avoid detection.

You should work on developing a strong, powerful yell for self-defense. A good place to practice is in the privacy of your car. Its interior insulates you and amplifies your voice to give you a good idea of its power. Work on making your yell loud and ferocious, like a lion. Let it rise from deep within your solar plexus. Practice prolonged yells and intermittent explosive ones. Finally, don't limit your yelling to raw primal sounds. Practice situational words like no, stop, hands off, and fire. Such words are ideal for a woman faced with a potential rapist.

Elbows

With very little training, you can learn to use your elbows as devastating self-defense weapons. They are explosive, deceptive, and difficult to stop. By rotating your body into the blow, you can generate tremendous force. You can deliver elbow strikes horizontally, vertically, and diagonally to the assailant's nose, temple, chin, throat, solar plexus, and ribs.

Fists

The fists are used for punching an assailant's temple, nose, chin, throat, solar plexus, ribs, and groin. However, punching with your fists is a true art, requiring considerable time and training to master. If your goal is short-term self-defense training, I suggest that you strike with the heel of your palm instead.

The Fingers/Nails

Your fingers and nails can be used for jabbing, gouging, and clawing a criminal's eyes. They can also be used for grabbing, pulling, tearing, and crushing his throat or testicles. To strengthen their fingernails, women should consider applying commercial nail-hardening liquid.

Palms

One alternative to punching with your fists is to strike with the heel of your palm. A palm strike from either one of your hands is very powerful and should always be delivered in an upward, thrusting motion to the assailant's nose or chin.

Edge of the Hand

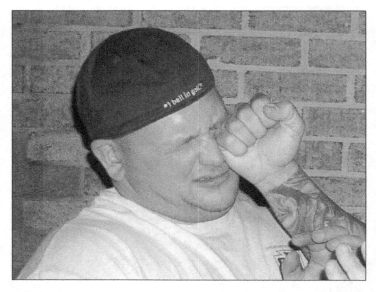

You can throw the edge of your hand in a whip-like motion to surprise and neutralize your attacker. By whipping your arm horizontally to his nose or throat, you can cause severe injury or death. The edge of your hand can also be thrown vertically or diagonally to the back of the assailant's neck as a finishing blow.

Web of Hand

The web of your hand can be used to deliver web hand strikes to the opponent's throat. When striking, be certain to keep your hand stiff with your palm facing down.

Knees

When you are knife fighting in close-quarter range, your knees can be extremely powerful weapons. You can deliver knee strikes vertically and diagonally to the assailant's thigh and groin, ribs, solar plexus, and face.

Shins

Striking with your shinbone can quickly cripple a powerful assailant and bring him to his knees in agony. That's right - your shinbone is a weapon. When striking with your shin, you can aim for his thigh, the side of his knee, or groin - and always remember to aim through your target.

Dorsum of Foot

You can use the dorsum of your foot to execute a vertical kick to the assailant's groin. Striking with the dorsum increases the power of your kick, prevents broken toes, and also lengthens the surface area of your strike.

Heel of the Foot

You can use the heel of your foot to execute a side kick to the criminal's knee or shin. When fighting an attacker in close quarter range, you can use the heel of your foot to stomp down on the assailant's instep or toes.

Ball of the Foot

You can use the ball of your foot to execute a push kick into the assailant's thigh. You can also snap it quickly into the assailant's shin to loosen a grab from the front. When striking the assailant with the ball of your foot, be certain to pull your toes back to avoid jamming or breaking them.

Bonus Knife Fighting Material

As you can imagine, edged weapon combat is a vast subject filled with numerous subtle details. So, I've included several more knife fighting techniques and strategies for you.

11. Accuracy is everything

Despite what some instructors might say, tactical knife fighting requires fine motor skills; you must be able to cut the criminal attacker with surgical precision. Accuracy is by far the most important attribute in edged weapon combat. If your cut is off target by as much as a fraction of an inch, you could turn a deadly attack into a superficial wound. The bottom line is you must be able to strike what you aim at. It is that simple folks!

12. Know why others prefer a rear hand knife stance

Despite the clear tactical advantages of holding your knife in your front hand, there are still other people who will still hold their weapon in their rear hand. Understanding these reasons can be a tremendous advantage for you and it's what I call *Understanding the Nature of the Beast*. What follows are some of the reasons for a rear hand knife stance.

1. **Protection** - their front hand is free to block or deflect any strikes launched against them.

2. **Grabbing** - their front hand is free to grab and pull victims off balance, thereby exposing vital targets.

3. **Distracting** - their front hand is free to cause feints or other distractions.

4. **Striking** - their front hand is used as a secondary weapon that can punch or strike at will.

13. Avoid clenching your knife too tightly

Knife fighting is a situation of dire consequences that puts your mind and body under a tremendous amount of stress. It's only natural that you will be tense. However, when assuming a knife fighting stance, make a conscious effort to avoid clenching your knife too tightly. Not only with this cause your veins to protrude from your arms, it will also inhibit your ability to manipulate the knife speed and efficiency.

14. Expect to get cut

Whether you're unarmed and defending against a knife attack or knife fighting with your adversary, expect to get cut. This frame of mind is critical for the following reasons:

1. It prepares you for the cold reality of edged-weapon combat.

2. It helps prevent you from going into mental shock if you do get cut.

3. It frees you from the fear, worry and mental concern of your well-being.

15. Ignore your wound

If you're ever cut in a knife fight, do not look at your wound. You must ignore it until the threat is eliminated. Actually, looking at your wound in the middle of a knife fight can be dangerous for the following four reasons:

1. It takes your eyes off of your immediate threat - the assailant and his knife.

2. It can psyche you out.

3. It may cause you to go into shock.

4. It will immediately empower your assailant.

16. Avoid judgment

When face to face with another knife fighter, don't assume you can judge his proficiency with a knife by the way he holds one. Always assume that anyone holding a knife (or any weapon for that matter) knows how to use it and will do just that. Besides, even if your assailant is unskilled as a knife fighter, he or she can still kill you.

17. Don't throw your knife

Contrary to what you may have seen on TV or in the movies, throwing your knife at your assailant is a dangerous idea for some of the following reasons:

1. Few knives are specifically designed and balanced for throwing movements.

2. It's extremely difficult to hit a moving target when throwing any type of knife.

3. If your knife misses its target, it will automatically arm your adversary with two knives.

4. Knife fighting will often takes place at close-quarters with very limited space. Knife throwing, on the other hand, requires an appreciable amount of distance between you and the adversary in order for the knife to generate the necessary power and velocity.

18. Don't shift your weight to your rear leg

When advancing in a knife fight, avoid shifting your weight to the rear leg prior to moving forward at your assailant. Shifting your weight back prior to moving forward will telegraph your movement, waste time, and propel you upward rather than forward.

19. Master drawing skills

Spend just as much time learning to draw your knife quickly as you would practicing your offensive and defensive knife fighting skills. Also avoid using the cross-draw technique, which allows your adversary the opportunity to immobilize your drawing arm temporarily.

20. Don't telegraph your cut

The element of surprise is invaluable when knife fighting. Successfully delivering a stash or a stab requires that you do not forewarn your assailant of your intentions. Clenching your teeth, widening your eyes, cocking knife back, and tensing your neck or shoulders are just a few common telegraphic cues that will negate the element of surprise.

One of the best ways to prevent telegraphic movement is to maintain a poker face prior to executing your attack. Avoid all facial expressions when faced with a threatening assailant. You can study your knife fighting techniques in front of a full-length mirror or have a friend videotape you performing your movements. These procedures will assist you in identifying and ultimately eliminating telegraphic movements. Be patient and you'll reach your objective.

21. Never forget what a knife fight really is

There are many words that accurately describe the nature and characteristics of a knife fight. Here are a few to keep in mind before you decide to engage in a knife fight:

- brutal
- vicious
- unpredictable
- unfair
- hazardous
- menacing
- precarious
- treacherous
- uncertain
- intimate
- quick
- swift
- nonstop
- variable
- cruel
- deadly
- fierce
- barbarous
- exhausting
- difficult
- ugly
- graceless
- grisly
- gruesome

The 10 Best Knife Fighting Techniques

Chapter Three
Knife Fighting Training Tips

Practice Makes Survivors

All the information in the world is useless unless you put it into action. Physical knife fighting practice is critical! Remember, practice makes perfect, and perfect makes survivors.

You'll need to perform your knife fighting techniques, maneuvers and tactic repeatedly in order to master them and ultimately make them instinctual. Therefore, you must set aside some time from your busy schedule to practice and refine your edged weapon skills. This will require some planning on your part.

Safe and Effective Knife Training

When it comes to knife fighting training, safety is of paramount importance. Unfortunately, some practitioners will avoid using safety equipment because of big egos, laziness, ignorance and a variety of other reasons. However, it behooves you to take the proper safety precautions.

Here are a few suggestions to help minimize the possibilities of injury when knife training:

1. Never, ever practice with real knives.

2. Buy the best knife training equipment that you can afford.

3. Have a trained expert show you the proper way to use the equipment.

4. Regularly inspect your training knife and eye protection for wear and defects.

5. Be especially alert when training with someone with superior skill or experience.

6. Be very cautions when performing knife training drills for the first time.

The 10 Best Knife Fighting Techniques

The only effective method of developing knife fighting skills is to practice safely with a training partner. There are numerous training knives on the market. When looking to purchase training knives, avoid buying those rubber knives that wiggle when you move them. These knives are cheap and very unrealistic.

Also, be exceptionally careful when slashing at your partner's face. To prevent eye injuries, wear some eye protection. Again, *never practice with real knives.*

If you are going to workout with a rubber training knife, be certain to use one that is made of hard rubber.

Realism is the key to your Survival

When training for knife fighting, your workouts must be completely realistic. Anything less could spell disaster for you when a real edged-weapon situation occurs. You must methodically integrate the frightening and spontaneous elements of combat safely into your workout routine. Such reality-based training is a sure fire method of preparing you for the real thing.

For example, frequently conduct simulated knife fights with your training partner using training knives and protective gear. Try to work out in cramped and unfamiliar environments. Train in the rain, in the snow, in the mud, etc.

Since no two knife fights are ever the same, you need to incorporate a wide variety of combative scenarios into your training program. This realistic and dynamic form of training will provide you with the experience necessary to handle the unpredictable nature of knife combat. Remember, inadequate or unrealistic training is a waste of time and extremely dangerous for you. Always train for the reality of combat.

Finally, when purchasing knife training gear, spare no expense. Edged weapon training is a serious matter, and your training gear should reflect it. Good equipment will provide years of reliable use and significantly enhance your skills.

If you are planning on practicing with tactical folders, Spyderco has produced some quality knives specifically for knife fighting training.

If you are planning on working on fixed blade training, there are several excellent rubber knives on the market.

Knife fighting drills and exercises

There are literally dozens of different knife fighting drills. Here are just a few exercises that can help you get a jump start on your training.

Mirror knife training

In front of a mirror, practice linear and lateral footwork movements with a training knife in your hand. This should be performed in both your right and left stances. Be aware of your stance as you move, keep your weight evenly distributed, keep your balance, and stay relaxed. This should be practiced on all different types of terrain (wet grass, mud, ice, wet pavement, snow, gravel, and sand).

You must also practice the knife fighting stance until it becomes instinctual. This means that you will have to practice in front of a full-length mirror. When you assume your stance, scrutinize yourself and pick out the strategic deficiencies. For example, what targets are exposed? Is your balance sacrificed? Are your knees bent?

Non-dominant hand knife training

When practicing knife fighting skills, always devote sufficient time to your non-dominant hand. As in unarmed combat, ambidexterity is an invaluable skill. Here are just a few reasons why it should be your weak hand should be developed:

1. There is a possibility that your strong hand might be injured in a knife fight and you will be forced to use your weak hand.

2. It enhances your overall combat confidence.

3. It reinforces good knife fighting skills.

4. It can be useful if your dominant hand becomes occupied during the knife fight.

Practice in close quarters

You should also spend adequate time learning how to use your knife in close-quarter environments. Here are just a few examples:

1. In your car.

2. In an elevator.

3. On a bridge.

4. In a narrow hallway.

5. In a doorway.

6. In a bathroom stall.

7. In a crowd.

8. In a cluttered garage.

9. On a narrow stairwell.

10. Between tall shrubbery

Knife retention training

There's a good possibility that a knife fight will end up in a struggle with the adversary. In fact, the vast majority of knife fighting simulations conducted in my school usually end up the two students struggling to hold on to their weapon.

This brings up the important issue of knife retention skills. Never pick up a knife unless you are absolutely confident that you can maintain complete control over it at all times. Remember, if you drop your knife, you might very well lose your life.

The bottom line is, a well-trained knife fighter must be adequately trained in knife-retention skills. He or she must know effective counters to various types of traps, grabs and disarm techniques.

Petroleum jelly

If you want to replicate the sweat, blood and grim that often accompanies a knife fight, rub a liberal amount of petroleum jelly on your hands prior to training. Not only will this test the integrity of your grip, it will also teach you how to improvise your knife fighting skills when faced with adverse conditions.

Just remember, this type of knife fighting training is very challenging and should only be used by experienced practitioners who possess a strong foundation in edged weapon combat.

Disability Training

Disability training is designed to help you experience what it's like to knife fight when you are under the weather or temporarily handicapped. Here are a few suggestions that will help get you started.

1. Practice when you're plagued with a migraine headache.

2. Practice knife fighting when confined to a wheelchair.

3. Knife spar with one arm in a sling.

4. Practice knife skills while standing on crutches.

5. Engage in ground knife fighting when you are feeling fatigued or exhausted.

6. Practice knife weapon retention while you are blindfolded.

7. Knife spar while wearing a weight vest.

8. Wear an elevation training mask when knife sparring.

9. Want to experience some real physical discomfort, practice knife training drills with a marble in your shoe.

10. Knife fight with you non-dominant hand against your partners dominant hand.

Videotaping your workouts

If you really want to actually see your progress, videotape your knife fighting workouts. The video footage will provide you with a more accurate picture of what you are doing in your training. You will be able to observe mistakes and recognize your strengths and weaknesses. The video will also motivate you to train harder. Remember to date each video clip; later on you will be able to compare and see marked improvements in your training performance.

Reading and Research

The intellectual, or academic, aspects of knife fighting training cannot be overstated. You must possess an insatiable desire to learn and grow to your full potential. Academic research involves voracious reading. The body of printed materials on knife fighting has grown astronomically.

Try to read anything you can get your hands on. However, don't make the common mistake of passively reading material. Get into the habit of dissecting and noting literature. Strategically sound knife fighting theories and unique training concepts should be noted and remembered. Books should be read over and over again until practical ideas are intellectually solidified. Finally, always read material with an open mind balanced with healthy skepticism.

Glossary

The following terms are defined in the context of Contemporary Fighting Arts and its related concepts. In many instances, the definitions bear little resemblance to those found in a standard dictionary.

A

accuracy—The precise or exact projection of force. Accuracy is also defined as the ability to execute a combative movement with precision and exactness.

adaptability—The ability to physically and psychologically adjust to new or different conditions or circumstances of combat.

advanced first-strike tools—Offensive techniques that are specifically used when confronted with multiple opponents.

aerobic exercise—Literally, "with air." Exercise that elevates the heart rate to a training level for a prolonged period of time, usually 30 minutes.

affective preparedness – One of the three components of preparedness. Affective preparedness means being emotionally, philosophically, and spiritually prepared for the strains of combat. See cognitive preparedness and psychomotor preparedness.

aggression—Hostile and injurious behavior directed toward a person.

aggressive response—One of the three possible counters when assaulted by a grab, choke, or hold from a standing position. Aggressive response requires you to counter the enemy with destructive blows and strikes. See moderate response and passive response.

aggressive hand positioning—Placement of hands so as to imply

The 10 Best Knife Fighting Techniques

aggressive or hostile intentions.

agility—An attribute of combat. One's ability to move his or her body quickly and gracefully.

amalgamation—A scientific process of uniting or merging.

ambidextrous—The ability to perform with equal facility on both the right and left sides of the body.

anabolic steroids – synthetic chemical compounds that resemble the male sex hormone testosterone. This performance-enhancing drug is known to increase lean muscle mass, strength, and endurance.

analysis and integration—One of the five elements of CFA's mental component. This is the painstaking process of breaking down various elements, concepts, sciences, and disciplines into their atomic parts, and then methodically and strategically analyzing, experimenting, and drastically modifying the information so that it fulfills three combative requirements: efficiency, effectiveness, and safety. Only then is it finally integrated into the CFA system.

anatomical striking targets—The various anatomical body targets that can be struck and which are especially vulnerable to potential harm. They include: the eyes, temple, nose, chin, back of neck, front of neck, solar plexus, ribs, groin, thighs, knees, shins, and instep.

anchoring – The strategic process of trapping the assailant's neck or limb in order to control the range of engagement during razing.

assailant—A person who threatens or attacks another person.

assault—The threat or willful attempt to inflict injury upon the person of another.

assault and battery—The unlawful touching of another person without justification.

assessment—The process of rapidly gathering, analyzing, and accurately evaluating information in terms of threat and danger. You can assess people, places, actions, and objects.

attack—Offensive action designed to physically control, injure, or kill another person.

attack by combination (ABC) - One of the five methods of attack. See compound attack.

attack by drawing (ABD) - One of the five methods of attack. A method of attack predicated on counterattack.

attitude—One of the three factors that determine who wins a street fight. Attitude means being emotionally, philosophically, and spiritually liberated from societal and religious mores. See skills and knowledge.

attributes of combat—The physical, mental, and spiritual qualities that enhance combat skills and tactics.

awareness—Perception or knowledge of people, places, actions, and objects. (In CFA, there are three categories of tactical awareness: criminal awareness, situational awareness, and self-awareness.)

B

balance—One's ability to maintain equilibrium while stationary or moving.

blading the body—Strategically positioning your body at a 45-degree angle.

blitz and disengage—A style of sparring whereby a fighter moves into a range of combat, unleashes a strategic compound attack, and then quickly disengages to a safe distance. Of all sparring methodologies, the blitz and disengage most closely resembles a real street fight.

block—A defensive tool designed to intercept the assailant's attack by placing a non-vital target between the assailant's strike and your vital body target.

body composition—The ratio of fat to lean body tissue.

body language—Nonverbal communication through posture, gestures, and facial expressions.

body mechanics—Technically precise body movement during the execution of a body weapon, defensive technique, or other fighting maneuver.

body tackle – A tackle that occurs when your opponent haphazardly rushes forward and plows his body into yours.

body weapon—Also known as a tool, one of the various body parts that can be used to strike or otherwise injure or kill a criminal assailant.

burn out—A negative emotional state acquired by physically over- training. Some symptoms include: illness, boredom, anxiety, disinterest in training, and general sluggishness.

C

cadence—Coordinating tempo and rhythm to establish a timing pattern of movement.

cardiorespiratory conditioning—The component of physical fitness that deals with the heart, lungs, and circulatory system.

centerline—An imaginary vertical line that divides your body in half and which contains many of your vital anatomical targets.

choke holds—Holds that impair the flow of blood or oxygen to the brain.

circular movements—Movements that follow the direction of a curve.

close-quarter combat—One of the three ranges of knife and

bludgeon combat. At this distance, you can strike, slash, or stab your assailant with a variety of close-quarter techniques.

cognitive development—One of the five elements of CFA's mental component. The process of developing and enhancing your fighting skills through specific mental exercises and techniques. See analysis and integration, killer instinct, philosophy, and strategic/tactical development.

cognitive exercises—Various mental exercises used to enhance fighting skills and tactics.

cognitive preparedness – One of the three components of preparedness. Cognitive preparedness means being equipped with the strategic concepts, principles, and general knowledge of combat. See affective preparedness and psychomotor preparedness.

combat-oriented training—Training that is specifically related to the harsh realities of both armed and unarmed combat. See ritual-oriented training and sport-oriented training.

combative arts—The various arts of war. See martial arts.

combative attributes—See attributes of combat.

combative fitness—A state characterized by cardiorespiratory and muscular/skeletal conditioning, as well as proper body composition.

combative mentality—Also known as the killer instinct, this is a combative state of mind necessary for fighting. See killer instinct.

combat ranges—The various ranges of unarmed combat.

combative utility—The quality of condition of being combatively useful.

combination(s)—See compound attack.

common peroneal nerve—A pressure point area located approximately four to six inches above the knee on the midline of the outside of the thigh.

composure—A combative attribute. Composure is a quiet and focused mind-set that enables you to acquire your combative agenda.

compound attack—One of the five conventional methods of attack. Two or more body weapons launched in strategic succession whereby the fighter overwhelms his assailant with a flurry of full speed, full-force blows.

conditioning training—A CFA training methodology requiring the practitioner to deliver a variety of offensive and defensive combinations for a 4-minute period. See proficiency training and street training.

contact evasion—Physically moving or manipulating your body to avoid being tackled by the adversary.

Contemporary Fighting Arts—A modern martial art and self-defense system made up of three parts: physical, mental, and spiritual.

conventional ground-fighting tools—Specific ground-fighting techniques designed to control, restrain, and temporarily incapacitate your adversary. Some conventional ground fighting tactics include: submission holds, locks, certain choking techniques, and specific striking techniques.

coordination—A physical attribute characterized by the ability to perform a technique or movement with efficiency, balance, and accuracy.

counterattack—Offensive action made to counter an assailant's initial attack.

courage—A combative attribute. The state of mind and spirit that enables a fighter to face danger and vicissitudes with confidence, resolution, and bravery.

creatine monohydrate—A tasteless and odorless white powder that mimics some of the effects of anabolic steroids. Creatine is a safe body-building product that can benefit anyone who wants to increase their strength, endurance, and lean muscle mass.

criminal awareness—One of the three categories of CFA awareness. It involves a general understanding and knowledge of the nature and dynamics of a criminal's motivations, mentalities, methods, and capabilities to perpetrate violent crime. See situational awareness and self-awareness.

criminal justice—The study of criminal law and the procedures associated with its enforcement.

criminology—The scientific study of crime and criminals.

cross-stepping—The process of crossing one foot in front of or behind the other when moving.

crushing tactics—Nuclear grappling-range techniques designed to crush the assailant's anatomical targets.

D

deadly force—Weapons or techniques that may result in unconsciousness, permanent disfigurement, or death.

deception—A combative attribute. A stratagem whereby you delude your assailant.

decisiveness—A combative attribute. The ability to follow a tactical course of action that is unwavering and focused.

defense—The ability to strategically thwart an assailant's attack (armed or unarmed).

defensive flow—A progression of continuous defensive responses.

defensive mentality—A defensive mind-set.

defensive reaction time—The elapsed time between an assailant's physical attack and your defensive response to that attack. See offensive reaction time.

demeanor—A person's outward behavior. One of the essential factors to consider when assessing a threatening individual.

diet—A lifestyle of healthy eating.

disingenuous vocalization—The strategic and deceptive utilization of words to successfully launch a preemptive strike at your adversary.

distancing—The ability to quickly understand spatial relationships and how they relate to combat.

distractionary tactics—Various verbal and physical tactics designed to distract your adversary.

double-end bag—A small leather ball hung from the ceiling and anchored to the floor with bungee cord. It helps develop striking accuracy, speed, timing, eye-hand coordination, footwork and overall defensive skills.

double-leg takedown—A takedown that occurs when your opponent shoots for both of your legs to force you to the ground.

E

ectomorph—One of the three somatotypes. A body type characterized by a high degree of slenderness, angularity, and fragility. See endomorph and mesomorph.

effectiveness—One of the three criteria for a CFA body weapon, technique, tactic, or maneuver. It means the ability to produce a desired effect. See efficiency and safety.

efficiency—One of the three criteria for a CFA body weapon, technique, tactic, or maneuver. It means the ability to reach an objective quickly and economically. See effectiveness and safety.

emotionless—A combative attribute. Being temporarily devoid of human feeling.

endomorph—One of the three somatotypes. A body type characterized by a high degree of roundness, softness, and body fat. See ectomorph and mesomorph.

evasion—A defensive maneuver that allows you to strategically maneuver your body away from the assailant's strike.

evasive sidestepping—Evasive footwork where the practitioner moves to either the right or left side.

evasiveness—A combative attribute. The ability to avoid threat or danger.

excessive force—An amount of force that exceeds the need for a particular event and is unjustified in the eyes of the law.

experimentation—The painstaking process of testing a combative hypothesis or theory.

explosiveness—A combative attribute that is characterized by a sudden outburst of violent energy.

F

fear—A strong and unpleasant emotion caused by the anticipation or awareness of threat or danger. There are three stages of fear in order of intensity: fright, panic, and terror. See fright, panic, and terror.

feeder—A skilled technician who manipulates the focus mitts.

femoral nerve—A pressure point area located approximately 6 inches above the knee on the inside of the thigh.

fighting stance—Any one of the stances used in CFA's system. A strategic posture you can assume when face-to-face with an unarmed assailant(s). The fighting stance is generally used after you have launched your first-strike tool.

fight-or-flight syndrome—A response of the sympathetic nervous system to a fearful and threatening situation, during which it prepares your body to either fight or flee from the perceived danger.

finesse—A combative attribute. The ability to skillfully execute a movement or a series of movements with grace and refinement.

first strike—Proactive force used to interrupt the initial stages of an assault before it becomes a self-defense situation.

first-strike principle—A CFA principle that states that when physical danger is imminent and you have no other tactical option but to fight back, you should strike first, strike fast, and strike with authority and keep the pressure on.

first-strike stance—One of the stances used in CFA's system. A strategic posture used prior to initiating a first strike.

first-strike tools—Specific offensive tools designed to initiate a preemptive strike against your adversary.

fisted blows – Hand blows delivered with a clenched fist.

five tactical options – The five strategic responses you can make in a self-defense situation, listed in order of increasing level of resistance: comply, escape, de-escalate, assert, and fight back.

flexibility—The muscles' ability to move through maximum natural ranges. See muscular/skeletal conditioning.

focus mitts—Durable leather hand mitts used to develop and sharpen offensive and defensive skills.

footwork—Quick, economical steps performed on the balls of the feet while you are relaxed, alert, and balanced. Footwork is structured around four general movements: forward, backward, right, and left.

fractal tool—Offensive or defensive tools that can be used in more than one combat range.

fright—The first stage of fear; quick and sudden fear. See panic and terror.

full Beat – One of the four beat classifications in the Widow Maker Program. The full beat strike has a complete initiation and retraction phase.

G

going postal - a slang term referring to a person who suddenly and unexpectedly attacks you with an explosive and frenzied flurry of blows. Also known as postal attack.

grappling range—One of the three ranges of unarmed combat. Grappling range is the closest distance of unarmed combat from which you can employ a wide variety of close-quarter tools and techniques. The grappling range of unarmed combat is also divided into two planes: vertical (standing) and horizontal (ground fighting). See kicking range and punching range.

grappling-range tools—The various body tools and techniques that are employed in the grappling range of unarmed combat, including head butts; biting, tearing, clawing, crushing, and gouging tactics; foot stomps, horizontal, vertical, and diagonal elbow strikes, vertical and diagonal knee strikes, chokes, strangles, joint locks, and holds. See punching range tools and kicking range tools.

ground fighting—Also known as the horizontal grappling plane, this is fighting that takes place on the ground.

guard—Also known as the hand guard, this refers to a fighter's hand positioning.

guard position—Also known as leg guard or scissors hold, this is a ground-fighting position in which a fighter is on his back holding his opponent between his legs.

H

half beat – One of the four beat classifications in the Widow Maker Program. The half beat strike is delivered through the retraction phase of the proceeding strike.

hand immobilization attack (HIA) - One of the five methods of attack. A method of attack whereby the practitioner traps his opponent's limb or limbs in order to execute an offense attack of his own.

hand positioning—See guard.

hand wraps—Long strips of cotton that are wrapped around the hands and wrists for greater protection.

haymaker—A wild and telegraphed swing of the arms executed by an unskilled fighter.

head-hunter—A fighter who primarily attacks the head.

heavy bag—A large cylindrical bag used to develop kicking, punching, or striking power.

high-line kick—One of the two different classifications of a kick. A kick that is directed to targets above an assailant's waist level. See low-line kick.

hip fusing—A full-contact drill that teaches a fighter to "stand his ground" and overcome the fear of exchanging blows with a stronger opponent. This exercise is performed by connecting two fighters with a 3-foot chain, forcing them to fight in the punching range of unarmed combat.

histrionics—The field of theatrics or acting.

hook kick—A circular kick that can be delivered in both kicking and punching ranges.

hook punch—A circular punch that can be delivered in both the punching and grappling ranges.

I

impact power—Destructive force generated by mass and velocity.

impact training—A training exercise that develops pain tolerance.

incapacitate—To disable an assailant by rendering him unconscious or damaging his bones, joints, or organs.

initiative—Making the first offensive move in combat.

inside position—The area between the opponent's arms, where he has the greatest amount of control.

intent—One of the essential factors to consider when assessing a threatening individual. The assailant's purpose or motive. See demeanor, positioning, range, and weapon capability.

intuition—The innate ability to know or sense something without the use of rational thought.

J

jeet kune do (JKD) - "Way of the intercepting fist." Bruce Lee's approach to the martial arts, which includes his innovative concepts, theories, methodologies, and philosophies.

jersey Pull - Strategically pulling the assailant's shirt or jacket over his head as he disengages from the clinch position.

joint lock—A grappling-range technique that immobilizes the assailant's joint.

K

kick—A sudden, forceful strike with the foot.

kicking range—One of the three ranges of unarmed combat. Kicking range is the furthest distance of unarmed combat wherein you use your legs to strike an assailant. See grappling range and punching range.

kicking-range tools—The various body weapons employed in the kicking range of unarmed combat, including side kicks, push kicks, hook kicks, and vertical kicks.

killer instinct—A cold, primal mentality that surges to your consciousness and turns you into a vicious fighter.

kinesics—The study of nonlinguistic body movement communications. (For example, eye movement, shrugs, or facial gestures.)

kinesiology—The study of principles and mechanics of human movement.

kinesthetic perception—The ability to accurately feel your body during the execution of a particular movement.

knowledge—One of the three factors that determine who will win a street fight. Knowledge means knowing and understanding how to fight. See skills and attitude.

L

lead side -The side of the body that faces an assailant.

leg guard—See guard position.

linear movement—Movements that follow the path of a straight line.

low-maintenance tool—Offensive and defensive tools that require the least amount of training and practice to maintain proficiency. Low maintenance tools generally do not require preliminary stretching.

low-line kick—One of the two different classifications of a kick. A kick that is directed to targets below the assailant's waist level. (See high-line kick.)

lock—See joint lock.

M

maneuver—To manipulate into a strategically desired position.

MAP—An acronym that stands for moderate, aggressive, passive. MAP provides the practitioner with three possible responses to various grabs, chokes, and holds that occur from a standing position. See aggressive response, moderate response, and passive response.

martial arts—The "arts of war."

masking—The process of concealing your true feelings from your opponent by manipulating and managing your body language.

mechanics—(See body mechanics.)

mental attributes—The various cognitive qualities that enhance your fighting skills.

mental component—One of the three vital components of the CFA system. The mental component includes the cerebral aspects of fighting including the killer instinct, strategic and tactical development, analysis and integration, philosophy, and cognitive development. See physical component and spiritual component.

mesomorph—One of the three somatotypes. A body type classified by a high degree of muscularity and strength. The mesomorph possesses the ideal physique for unarmed combat. See ectomorph and endomorph.

mobility—A combative attribute. The ability to move your body quickly and freely while balanced. See footwork.

moderate response—One of the three possible counters when assaulted by a grab, choke, or hold from a standing position. Moderate response requires you to counter your opponent with a control and restraint (submission hold). See aggressive response and passive response.

modern martial art—A pragmatic combat art that has evolved to meet the demands and characteristics of the present time.

mounted position—A dominant ground-fighting position where a fighter straddles his opponent.

muscular endurance—The muscles' ability to perform the same motion or task repeatedly for a prolonged period of time.

muscular flexibility—The muscles' ability to move through maximum natural ranges.

muscular strength—The maximum force that can be exerted by a particular muscle or muscle group against resistance.

muscular/skeletal conditioning—An element of physical fitness that entails muscular strength, endurance, and flexibility.

N

naked choke—A throat choke executed from the chest to back position. This secure choke is executed with two hands and it can be performed while standing, kneeling, and ground fighting with the opponent.

neck crush – A powerful pain compliance technique used when the adversary buries his head in your chest to avoid being razed.

neutralize—See incapacitate.

neutral zone—The distance outside the kicking range at which neither the practitioner nor the assailant can touch the other.

nonaggressive physiology—Strategic body language used prior to initiating a first strike.

nontelegraphic movement—Body mechanics or movements that do not inform an assailant of your intentions.

nuclear ground-fighting tools—Specific grappling range tools designed to inflict immediate and irreversible damage. Nuclear tools and tactics include biting tactics, tearing tactics, crushing tactics, continuous choking tactics, gouging techniques, raking tactics, and all striking techniques.

O

offense—The armed and unarmed means and methods of attacking a criminal assailant.

offensive flow—Continuous offensive movements (kicks, blows, and strikes) with unbroken continuity that ultimately neutralize or terminate the opponent. See compound attack.

offensive reaction time—The elapsed time between target selection and target impaction.

one-mindedness—A state of deep concentration wherein you are free from all distractions (internal and external).

ostrich defense—One of the biggest mistakes one can make when defending against an opponent. This is when the practitioner looks away from that which he fears (punches, kicks, and strikes). His mentality is, "If I can't see it, it can't hurt me."

P

pain tolerance—Your ability to physically and psychologically withstand pain.

panic—The second stage of fear; overpowering fear. See fright and terror.

parry—A defensive technique: a quick, forceful slap that redirects an assailant's linear attack. There are two types of parries: horizontal and vertical.

passive response—One of the three possible counters when assaulted by a grab, choke, or hold from a standing position. Passive response requires you to nullify the assault without injuring your adversary. See aggressive response and moderate response.

patience—A combative attribute. The ability to endure and tolerate difficulty.

perception—Interpretation of vital information acquired from your senses when faced with a potentially threatening situation.

philosophical resolution—The act of analyzing and answering various questions concerning the use of violence in defense of yourself and others.

philosophy—One of the five aspects of CFA's mental component. A deep state of introspection whereby you methodically resolve critical questions concerning the use of force in defense of yourself or others.

physical attributes—The numerous physical qualities that enhance your combative skills and abilities.

physical component—One of the three vital components of the CFA system. The physical component includes the physical aspects of fighting, such as physical fitness, weapon/technique mastery, and combative attributes. See mental component and spiritual component.

physical conditioning—See combative fitness.

physical fitness—See combative fitness.

positional asphyxia—The arrangement, placement, or positioning of your opponent's body in such a way as to interrupt your breathing and cause unconsciousness or possibly death.

positioning—The spatial relationship of the assailant to the assailed person in terms of target exposure, escape, angle of attack, and various other strategic considerations.

postal attack - see going postal.

power—A physical attribute of armed and unarmed combat. The amount of force you can generate when striking an anatomical target.

power generators—Specific points on your body that generate impact power. There are three anatomical power generators: shoulders, hips, and feet.

precision—See accuracy.

preemptive strike—See first strike.

premise—An axiom, concept, rule, or any other valid reason to modify or go beyond that which has been established.

preparedness—A state of being ready for combat. There are three components of preparedness: affective preparedness, cognitive preparedness, and psychomotor preparedness.

probable reaction dynamics - The opponent's anticipated or predicted movements or actions during both armed and unarmed combat.

proficiency training—A CFA training methodology requiring the practitioner to execute a specific body weapon, technique, maneuver, or tactic over and over for a prescribed number of repetitions. See conditioning training and street training.

progressive indirect attack (PIA) – One of the five methods of attack. A progressive method of attack whereby the initial tool or technique is designed to set the opponent up for follow-up blows.

proxemics—The study of the nature and effect of man's personal space.

The 10 Best Knife Fighting Techniques

proximity—The ability to maintain a strategically safe distance from a threatening individual.

pseudospeciation—A combative attribute. The tendency to assign subhuman and inferior qualities to a threatening assailant.

psychological conditioning—The process of conditioning the mind for the horrors and rigors of real combat.

psychomotor preparedness—One of the three components of preparedness. Psychomotor preparedness means possessing all of the physical skills and attributes necessary to defeat a formidable adversary. See affective preparedness and cognitive preparedness.

punch—A quick, forceful strike of the fists.

punching range—One of the three ranges of unarmed combat. Punching range is the mid range of unarmed combat from which the fighter uses his hands to strike his assailant. See kicking range and grappling range.

punching-range tools—The various body weapons that are employed in the punching range of unarmed combat, including finger jabs, palm-heel strikes, rear cross, knife-hand strikes, horizontal and shovel hooks, uppercuts, and hammer-fist strikes. See grappling-range tools and kicking-range tools.

Q

qualities of combat—See attributes of combat.

quarter beat - One of the four beat classifications of the Widow Maker Program. Quarter beat strikes never break contact with the assailant's face. Quarter beat strikes are primarily responsible for creating the psychological panic and trauma when Razing.

R

range—The spatial relationship between a fighter and a threatening assailant.

range deficiency—The inability to effectively fight and defend in all ranges of combat (armed and unarmed).

range manipulation—A combative attribute. The strategic manipulation of combat ranges.

range proficiency—A combative attribute. The ability to effectively fight and defend in all ranges of combat (armed and unarmed).

ranges of engagement—See combat ranges.

ranges of unarmed combat—The three distances (kicking range, punching range, and grappling range) a fighter might physically engage with an assailant while involved in unarmed combat.

raze – To level, demolish or obliterate.

razer – One who performs the Razing methodology.

razing – The second phase of the Widow Maker Program. A series of vicious close quarter techniques designed to physically and psychologically extirpate a criminal attacker.

razing amplifier - a technique, tactic or procedure that magnifies the destructiveness of your razing technique.

reaction dynamics—see probable reaction dynamics.

reaction time—The elapsed time between a stimulus and the response to that particular stimulus. See offensive reaction time and defensive reaction time.

rear cross—A straight punch delivered from the rear hand that crosses from right to left (if in a left stance) or left to right (if in a right stance).

rear side—The side of the body furthest from the assailant. See lead side.

reasonable force—That degree of force which is not excessive for a particular event and which is appropriate in protecting yourself or others.

refinement—The strategic and methodical process of improving or perfecting.

relocation principle—Also known as relocating, this is a street-fighting tactic that requires you to immediately move to a new location (usually by flanking your adversary) after delivering a compound attack.

repetition—Performing a single movement, exercise, strike, or action continuously for a specific period.

research—A scientific investigation or inquiry.

rhythm—Movements characterized by the natural ebb and flow of related elements.

ritual-oriented training—Formalized training that is conducted without intrinsic purpose. See combat-oriented training and sport-oriented training.

S

safety—One of the three criteria for a CFA body weapon, technique, maneuver, or tactic. It means that the tool, technique, maneuver or tactic provides the least amount of danger and risk for the practitioner. See efficiency and effectiveness.

scissors hold—See guard position.

scorching – Quickly and inconspicuously applying oleoresin capsicum (hot pepper extract) on your fingertips and then razing your adversary.

self-awareness—One of the three categories of CFA awareness. Knowing and understanding yourself. This includes aspects of yourself which may provoke criminal violence and which will promote a proper and strong reaction to an attack. See criminal awareness and situational awareness.

self-confidence—Having trust and faith in yourself.

self-enlightenment—The state of knowing your capabilities, limitations, character traits, feelings, general attributes, and motivations. See self-awareness.

set—A term used to describe a grouping of repetitions.

shadow fighting—A CFA training exercise used to develop and refine your tools, techniques, and attributes of armed and unarmed combat.

sharking – A counter attack technique that is used when your adversary grabs your razing hand.

shielding wedge - a defensive maneuver used to counter an unarmed postal attack.

simple direct attack (SDA) – One of the five methods of attack. A method of attack whereby the practitioner delivers a solitary offenses tool or technique. It may involve a series of discrete probes or one swift, powerful strike aimed at terminating the encounter.

situational awareness—One of the three categories of CFA awareness. A state of being totally alert to your immediate surroundings, including people, places, objects, and actions. (See criminal awareness and self-awareness.)

skeletal alignment—The proper alignment or arrangement of your body. Skeletal alignment maximizes the structural integrity of striking tools.

skills—One of the three factors that determine who will win a street fight. Skills refers to psychomotor proficiency with the tools and techniques of combat. See Attitude and Knowledge.

slipping—A defensive maneuver that permits you to avoid an assailant's linear blow without stepping out of range. Slipping can be accomplished by quickly snapping the head and upper torso sideways (right or left) to avoid the blow.

snap back—A defensive maneuver that permits you to avoid an assailant's linear and circular blows without stepping out of range. The snap back can be accomplished by quickly snapping the head backward to avoid the assailant's blow.

somatotypes—A method of classifying human body types or builds into three different categories: endomorph, mesomorph, and ectomorph. See endomorph, mesomorph, and ectomorph.

sparring—A training exercise where two or more fighters fight each other while wearing protective equipment.

speed—A physical attribute of armed and unarmed combat. The rate or a measure of the rapid rate of motion.

spiritual component—One of the three vital components of the CFA system. The spiritual component includes the metaphysical issues and aspects of existence. See physical component and mental component.

sport-oriented training—Training that is geared for competition and governed by a set of rules. See combat-oriented training and ritual-oriented training.

sprawling—A grappling technique used to counter a double- or single-leg takedown.

square off—To be face-to-face with a hostile or threatening assailant who is about to attack you.

stance—One of the many strategic postures you assume prior to or during armed or unarmed combat.

stick fighting—Fighting that takes place with either one or two sticks.

strategic positioning—Tactically positioning yourself to either escape, move behind a barrier, or use a makeshift weapon.

strategic/tactical development—One of the five elements of CFA's mental component.

strategy—A carefully planned method of achieving your goal of engaging an assailant under advantageous conditions.

street fight—A spontaneous and violent confrontation between two or more individuals wherein no rules apply.

street fighter—An unorthodox combatant who has no formal training. His combative skills and tactics are usually developed in the street by the process of trial and error.

street training—A CFA training methodology requiring the practitioner to deliver explosive compound attacks for 10 to 20 seconds. See condition ng training and proficiency training.

strength training—The process of developing muscular strength through systematic application of progressive resistance.

striking art—A combat art that relies predominantly on striking techniques to neutralize or terminate a criminal attacker.

striking shield—A rectangular shield constructed of foam and vinyl used to develop power in your kicks, punches, and strikes.

striking tool—A natural body weapon that impacts with the assailant's anatomical target.

strong side—The strongest and most coordinated side of your body.

structure—A definite and organized pattern.

style—The distinct manner in which a fighter executes or performs his combat skills.

stylistic integration—The purposeful and scientific collection of tools and techniques from various disciplines, which are strategically integrated and dramatically altered to meet three essential criteria: efficiency, effectiveness, and combative safety.

submission holds—Also known as control and restraint techniques, many of these locks and holds create sufficient pain to cause the adversary to submit.

system—The unification of principles, philosophies, rules, strategies, methodologies, tools, and techniques of a particular method of combat.

T

tactic—The skill of using the available means to achieve an end.

target awareness—A combative attribute that encompasses five strategic principles: target orientation, target recognition, target selection, target impaction, and target exploitation.

target exploitation—A combative attribute. The strategic maximization of your assailant's reaction dynamics during a fight. Target exploitation can be applied in both armed and unarmed encounters.

target impaction—The successful striking of the appropriate anatomical target.

target orientation—A combative attribute. Having a workable knowledge of the assailant's anatomical targets.

target recognition—The ability to immediately recognize appropriate anatomical targets during an emergency self-defense situation.

target selection—The process of mentally selecting the appropriate anatomical target for your self-defense situation. This is predicated on certain factors, including proper force response, assailant's positioning, and range.

target stare—A form of telegraphing in which you stare at the anatomical target you intend to strike.

target zones—The three areas in which an assailant's anatomical targets are located. (See zone one, zone two and zone three.)

technique—A systematic procedure by which a task is accomplished.

telegraphic cognizance—A combative attribute. The ability to recognize both verbal and non-verbal signs of aggression or assault.

telegraphing—Unintentionally making your intentions known to your adversary.

tempo—The speed or rate at which you speak.

terminate—To kill.

terror—The third stage of fear; defined as overpowering fear. See fright and panic.

timing—A physical and mental attribute of armed and unarmed combat. Your ability to execute a movement at the optimum moment.

tone—The overall quality or character of your voice.

tool—See body weapon.

traditional martial arts—Any martial art that fails to evolve and change to meet the demands and characteristics of its present environment.

traditional style/system—See traditional martial arts.

training drills—The various exercises and drills aimed at perfecting combat skills, attributes, and tactics.

trap and tuck – A counter move technique used when the adversary attempts to raze you during your quarter beat assault.

U

unified mind—A mind free and clear of distractions and focused on the combative situation.

use of force response—A combative attribute. Selecting the appropriate level of force for a particular emergency self-defense situation.

V

viciousness—A combative attribute. The propensity to be extremely violent and destructive often characterized by intense savagery.

violence—The intentional utilization of physical force to coerce, injure, cripple, or kill.

visualization—Also known as mental visualization or mental imagery. The purposeful formation of mental images and scenarios in the mind's eye.

W

warm-up—A series of mild exercises, stretches, and movements designed to prepare you for more intense exercise.

weak side—The weaker and more uncoordinated side of your body.

weapon and technique mastery—A component of CFA's physical component. The kinesthetic and psychomotor development of a weapon or combative technique.

weapon capability—An assailant's ability to use and attack with a particular weapon.

webbing - The first phase of the Widow Maker Program. Webbing is a two hand strike delivered to the assailant's chin. It is called Webbing because your hands resemble a large web that wraps around the enemy's face.

widow maker – One who makes widows by destroying husbands.

widow maker program – A CFA combat program specifically designed to teach the law abiding citizen how to use extreme force when faced with immediate threat of unlawful deadly criminal attack. The Widow Maker program is divided into two phases or methodologies: Webbing and Razing.

Y

yell—A loud and aggressive scream or shout used for various strategic reasons.

Z

zero beat – One of the four beat classifications of the Widow Maker, Feral Fighting and Savage Street Fighting Programs. Zero beat strikes are full pressure techniques applied to a specific target until it completely ruptures. They include gouging, crushing, biting, and choking techniques.

zone one—Anatomical targets related to your senses, including the eyes, temple, nose, chin, and back of neck.

zone three—Anatomical targets related to your mobility, including thighs, knees, shins, and instep.

zone two—Anatomical targets related to your breathing, including front of neck, solar plexus, ribs, and groin.

The 10 Best Knife Fighting Techniques

About Sammy Franco

With over 30 years of experience, Sammy Franco is one of the world's foremost authorities on armed and unarmed self-defense. Highly regarded as a leading innovator in combat sciences, Mr. Franco was one of the premier pioneers in the field of "reality-based" self-defense and martial arts instruction.

Sammy Franco is perhaps best known as the founder and creator of Contemporary Fighting Arts (CFA), a state-of-the-art offensive-based combat system that is specifically designed for real-world self-defense. CFA is a sophisticated and practical system of self-defense, designed specifically to provide efficient and effective methods to avoid, defuse, confront, and neutralize both armed and unarmed attackers.

Sammy Franco has frequently been featured in martial art magazines, newspapers, and appeared on numerous radio and television programs. Mr. Franco has also authored numerous books, magazine articles, and editorials, and has developed a popular library of instructional videos.

Sammy Franco's experience and credibility in the combat sciences is unequaled. One of his many accomplishments in this field includes the fact that he has earned the ranking of a Law Enforcement Master Instructor, and has designed, implemented, and taught officer survival training to the United States Border Patrol (USBP). He has instructed members of the US Secret Service, Military Special Forces,

The 10 Best Knife Fighting Techniques

Washington DC Police Department, Montgomery County, Maryland Deputy Sheriffs, and the US Library of Congress Police. Sammy Franco is also a member of the prestigious International Law Enforcement Educators and Trainers Association (ILEETA) as well as the American Society of Law Enforcement Trainers (ASLET) and he is listed in the "Who's Who Director of Law Enforcement Instructors."

Sammy Franco is a nationally certified Law Enforcement Instructor in the following curricula: PR-24 Side-Handle Baton, Police Arrest and Control Procedures, Police Personal Weapons Tactics, Police Power Handcuffing Methods, Police Oleoresin Capsicum Aerosol Training (OCAT), Police Weapon Retention and Disarming Methods, Police Edged Weapon Countermeasures and "Use of Force" Assessment and Response Methods.

Mr. Franco holds a Bachelor of Arts degree in Criminal Justice from the University of Maryland. He is a regularly featured speaker at a number of professional conferences and conducts dynamic and enlightening seminars on numerous aspects of self-defense and combat training.

On a personal level, Sammy Franco is an animal lover, who will go to great lengths to assist and rescue animals. Throughout the years, he's rescued everything from turkey vultures to goats. However, his most treasured moments are always spent with his beloved German Shepherd dogs.

For more information about Mr. Franco and his unique Contemporary Fighting Arts system, you can visit his website at: **SammyFranco.com** or follow him on twitter **@RealSammyFranco**

Other Books by Sammy Franco

SURVIVAL WEAPONS
A User's Guide to the Best Self-Defense Weapons for Surviving Any Dangerous Situation
by Sammy Franco

Whether you are just commuting around town or preparing for a SHTF scenario, Survival Weapons: A User's Guide to the Best Self-Defense Weapons for Surviving Any Dangerous Situation teaches you how to choose with the most efficient weapons for any survival situation. A must-have book for anyone interested in real world survival and wants to dramatically improve their odds of prevailing in any high-risk combat situation. 8.5 x 5.5, paperback, photos, illus, 210 pages.

CANE FIGHTING
The Authoritative Guide to Using the Cane or Walking Stick for Self-Defense
by Sammy Franco

Cane Fighting: The Authoritative Guide to Using the Cane or Walking Stick for Self-Defense is a no nonsense book written for anyone who wants to learn how to use the cane or walking stick as a fighting weapon for real-world self-defense. With over 200 photographs and step-by-step instructions, Cane Fighting is the authoritative resource for mastering the Hooked Wooden Cane, Modern Tactical Combat Cane, Walking Sticks, Irish Fighting Shillelagh and the Bo Staff: 8.5 x 5.5, paperback, photos, illus, 242 pages.

KNOCKOUT
The Ultimate Guide to Sucker Punching
by Sammy Franco

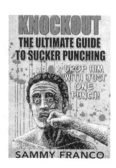

Knockout is a one-of-a-kind book designed to teach you the lost art and science of sucker punching for real-world self-defense situations. With over 150 detailed photographs, 244 pages and dozens of easy-to-follow instructions, Knockout has everything you need to master the devastating art of sucker punching. Whether you are a beginner or advanced, student or teacher, Knockout teaches you brutally effective skills, battle-tested techniques, and proven strategies to get you home alive and in one piece. 8.5 x 5.5, paperback, 244 pages.

SAVAGE STREET FIGHTING
Tactical Savagery as a Last Resort
by Sammy Franco

In this revolutionary book, Sammy Franco reveals the science behind his most primal street fighting method. Savage Street Fighting is a brutal self-defense system specifically designed to teach the law-abiding citizen how to use "Tactical Savagery" when faced with the immediate threat of an unlawful deadly criminal attack. Savage Street Fighting is systematically engineered to protect you when there are no other self-defense options left! With over 300 photographs and detailed step-by-step instructions, Savage Street Fighting is a must-have book for anyone concerned about real world self-defense. Now is the time to learn how to unleash your inner beast! 8.5 x 5.5, paperback, 317 photos, illustrations, 232 pages.

FIRST STRIKE
End a Fight in Ten Seconds or Less!
by Sammy Franco

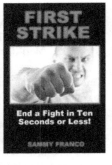

Learn how to stop any attack before it starts by mastering the art of the preemptive strike. First Strike gives you an easy-to-learn yet highly effective self-defense game plan for handling violent close-quarter combat encounters. First Strike will teach you instinctive, practical and realistic self-defense techniques that will drop any criminal attacker to the floor with one punishing blow. By reading this book and by practicing, you will learn the hard-hitting skills necessary to execute a punishing first strike and ultimately prevail in a self-defense situation. And that's what it is all about: winning in as little time as possible. 8.5 x 5.5, paperback, photos, illustrations, 202 pages.

WAR MACHINE
How to Transform Yourself Into A Vicious & Deadly Street Fighter
by Sammy Franco

War Machine is a book that will change you for the rest of your life! When followed accordingly, War Machine will forge your mind, body and spirit into iron. Once armed with the mental and physical attributes of the War Machine, you will become a strong and confident warrior that can handle just about anything that life may throw your way. In essence, War Machine is a way of life. Powerful, intense, and hard. 11 x 8.5, paperback, photos, illustrations, 210 pages.

KUBOTAN POWER
Quick and Simple Steps to Mastering the Kubotan Keychain
by Sammy Franco

With over 290 photographs and step-by-step instructions, Kubotan Power is the authoritative resource for mastering this devastating self-defense weapon. In this one-of-a-kind book, world-renowned self-defense expert, Sammy Franco takes thirty years of real-world teaching experience and gives you quick, easy and practical kubotan techniques that can be used by civilians, law enforcement personnel, or military professionals. The Kubotan is an incredible self-defense weapon that has helped thousands of people effectively defend themselves. Men, women, law enforcement officers, military, and security professionals alike, appreciate this small and discreet self-defense tool. Unfortunately, however, very little has been written about the kubotan, leaving it shrouded in both mystery and ignorance. As a result, most people don't know how to unleash the full power of this unique personal defense weapon. 8.5 x 5.5, paperback, 290 photos, illustrations, 204 pages.

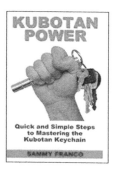

THE COMPLETE BODY OPPONENT BAG BOOK
by Sammy Franco

In this one-of-a-kind book, Sammy Franco teaches you the many hidden training features of the body opponent bag that will improve your fighting skills and boost your conditioning. With detailed photographs, step-by-step instructions, and dozens of unique workout routines, The Complete Body Opponent Bag Book is the authoritative resource for mastering this lifelike punching bag. The Complete Body Opponent Bag Book covers stances, punching, kicking, grappling techniques, mobility and footwork, targets, fighting ranges, training gear, time based workouts, punching and kicking combinations, weapons training, grappling drills, ground fighting, and dozens of workouts that will challenge you for years to come. 8.5 x 5.5, paperback, 139 photos, illustrations, 206 pages.

CONTEMPORARY FIGHTING ARTS
"Real World Self-Defense Since 1989"
SammyFranco.com

Made in the USA
Las Vegas, NV
13 September 2023

77523550R00085